ISAAC THE PIRATE
1. To Exotic Lands

D1294034

Also available by Christophe Blain:
The Speed Abater, $13.95
Dungeon Early Years, $14.95
Isaac The Pirate: Vol. 2, $14.95
($3 P&H 1st item, $1 each addt'l)

We have over 200 graphic novels in stock, ask for
our color catalog:
NBM
555 8th Ave., Suite 1202
New York, NY 10018
www.nbmpublishing.com

ISAAC THE PIRATE

1. To Exotic Lands

Christophe Blain

7/11

nbm ComicsLit

ISBN 1-56163-366-6
© Dargaud, 2001, 2002
© NBM 2003 for the English translation
Published first in French in two parts (*Les Ameriques and Les Glaces*)
Translation by Joe Johnson
Lettering by Ortho
Printed in China

3   2

Library of Congress Cataloging-in-Publication Data

Blain, Christophe.
    [Isaac le pirate. English]
    Isaac the pirate / Christophe Blain ; [translation by Joe Johnson].
        p. cm.
    Contents: v. 1. To exotic lands.
    ISBN 1-56163-366-6 (v. 1 : pbk.)
    I. Title.

PN6747.B58I8313 2003
741.5'944--dc22
                                                            2003059288

Comicslit is an imprint
and trademark of

NANTIER · BEALL · MINOUSTCHINE
Publishing inc.
new york

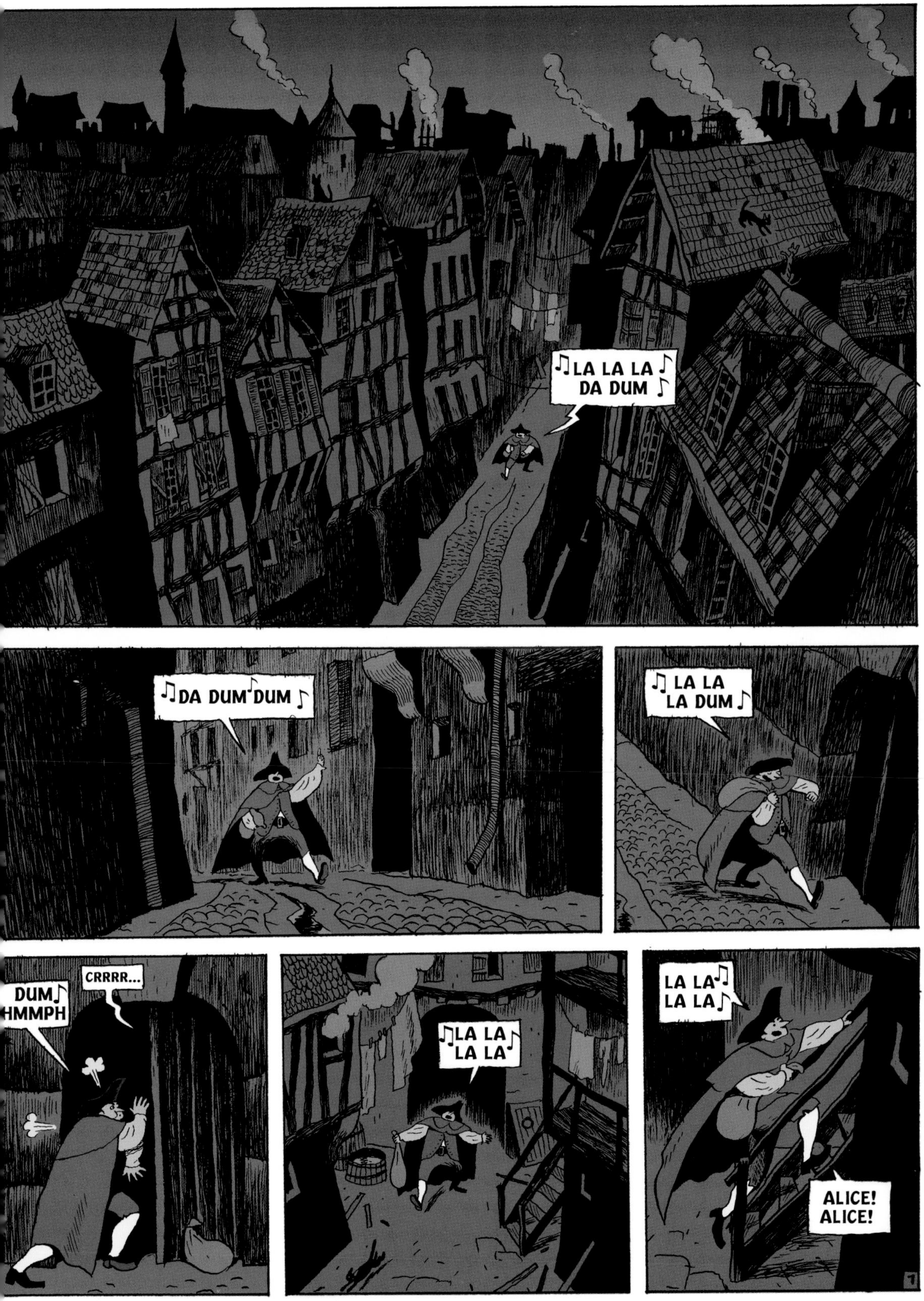

♫LA LA LA♪
DA DUM♪
♫DA DUM♪DUM♪
♫LA LA
LA DUM♪
DUM♪
HMMPH
CRRRR...
♫LA LA♪
LA LA♪
LA LA♫
LA LA♪
ALICE!
ALICE!
7

OPEN UP, SWEETIE!

BOOM! BOOM!

EVENIN', DARLING!

UH OH! MR. AUBRAN HAS LOANED YOU ANOTHER BIG BOOK. WHEN ARE YOU GOING TO STOP TEASING THAT DIRTY OLD MAN JUST TO RANSACK HIS LIBRARY?

GIVE IT BACK!

HMM! WHAT'S IT ABOUT THIS TIME? THE OSTROGOTHS? PAPOOSES? PICKLES?

THE KIKUYUS, THEY'RE A TRIBE FROM THE ANTIPODES COMPRISED OF VERY INTELLIGENT, SCIENTIFIC PEOPLE. MORE INTELLIGENT THAN YOU!

A GREAT DUTCH EXPLORER WROTE IT. THE KIKUYUS HAVE A HIGHLY EVOLVED LANGUAGE AND CUSTOMS.

ONE DAY, I'LL COME HOME AND YOU'LL HAVE LEARNED THE LANGUAGE OF THE ELVES THAT LIVE ATOP THE TREES OF ORIENTAL FORESTS.

EXACTLY! THEN I'LL LEAVE YOU TO GO LIVE AMONGST THEM, BECAUSE THEY'RE GENTLE, REFINED FOLK!

LOOK! LOOK! I'M AN ELF AND I SPEAK THE LANGUAGE OF THE FOREST: QUACK! QUACK! QUACK!

IN THE MEANTIME, WE'LL HAVE SOMETHING TO EAT EVERY DAY! MR. BOWLE, THE NOTARY, HAS AGREED FOR ME TO HELP HIM. HE'LL GIVE ME A PENNY FOR EVERY LINE I WRITE.

HUH? WHAT? ARE YOU FLIRTING WITH THAT OLD BASTARD, TOO?

WHO'S TALKING ABOUT FOOD? LOOK WHAT I BROUGHT BACK, DEAR: SOME SMOKED HAM, SAUSAGE, BREAD, CHEESE, TOMATOES, ITALIAN WINE. THAT ITALIAN GUY DELPIANO GAVE IT ALL TO ME BECAUSE I PAINTED HIS SIGN AND HE THOUGHT IT WAS "SOOPERBA".

HE SAID IT'D BRING IN LOTS OF CUSTOMERS.

LET'S EAT RIGHT AWAY! IT'S VERY BAD FOR YOUR HEALTH TO BE SO HUNGRY. EVER SINCE MY FATHER STOPPED GIVING US MONEY, I'VE LOST AT LEAST FIFTEEN POUNDS!

ISAAC! YOUR FATHER AND YOU HAVE HAD A FALLING OUT FOR ONLY THREE DAYS

YOU KNOW VERY WELL I GET SKINNY WHEN I'M WORRIED.

YOU'D HAVE A FEW LESS WORRIES IF YOU'D AGREED TO JOIN LONNAIRE'S STUDIO.

TO HAVE AS MY MASTER AN OLD FOP WHO PAINTS CRAP? THANKS, YOU'VE GOT A LOW OPINION OF YOUR MAN!

HE'S THIRTY YEARS OLDER THAN I, BUT CAN'T DO HALF AS MUCH AS I CAN. I'LL BE A FAMOUS PAINTER BEFORE HE DIES AND I'LL GO MAKE FUN OF HIM.

FORGET LONNAIRE! IT'S DONE RAINING AND I FEEL HAPPY. IT'S STILL WARM OUT.

SO, ALL DONE WITH YOUR BAD MOOD?

WHAT? I WASN'T IN SUCH A BAD MOOD! YOU KNOW I SOMETIMES HAVE TO WORK THINGS OUT A LITTLE.

WHAT WERE YOU SINGING JUST NOW AS YOU ARRIVED? IT MADE ME WANT TO DANCE.

DUM DUM ♪LA LA♪

YES, THAT'S IT.

♪ SO LET'S DANCE! DA DUM DA DUM ♪

WE SHOULD DANCE MORE OFTEN!

♪DUM DUM DUM♪

EVERY TIME I'M HAPPY. LIKE RIGHT NOW.

I'VE GOT A BETTER IDEA! I'M GOING TO PAINT YOU! GET NAKED!

RIGHT NOW? CAN'T WAIT TILL TOMORROW?

NO! NO! I FEEL GOOD TONIGHT. I'VE NOT PAINTED IN OVER A WEEK, AND I NEED TO KNOW IF I STILL CAN DRAW AND PAINT, OTHERWISE I'LL SLEEP POORLY! YOU GO READ NAKED ON THE BED, AND I'LL PAINT YOU.

DARLING? IS IT TRUE I'VE BEEN A PAIN THIS WEEK? DON'T MOVE!

YOU WERE AWFUL!

NO, NO! DON'T GIVE ME A GUILT TRIP! I NEED FOR YOU TO LEAVE ME WONDERING. IF I FEEL GUILTY FOR BOTHERING YOU WITH MY MOOD SWINGS, I'LL FEEL THAT MUCH WORSE THEN I CAN'T DRAW OR PAINT ANY MORE OR DO ANYTHING ELSE.

I LET YOU FUSS AND PUT ON A SULK WITHOUT COMPLAINT, RIGHT?

YES! YES! THAT'S RIGHT! ANYWAY, YOU KNOW VERY WELL I NEVER MEAN WHAT I SAY AT THE TIME, AND THAT I'M ALWAYS SORRY AFTERWARDS.

DON'T WORRY, MY LOVE, SOON EVERY- BODY WILL RECOGNIZE YOU'RE A GENIUS!

DON'T MAKE FUN OF ME AND LET ME SKETCH YOU.

ISAAC? DO YOU THINK YOUR FATHER WILL LET US MARRY?

I DON'T GIVE A DAMN WHAT HE THINKS. YOU'LL BE MY WIFE!

MAYBE I COULD CONVERT?

NO! I WANT TO MARRY YOU! YOU'RE A GENTILE AND I WANT TO MARRY A GENTILE!

NEITHER YOU NOR HIM CAN GO ON BEING MAD FOR LONG, ISAAC. YOUR FATHER'S A GOOD MAN.

HUSH! I DON'T WANT TO TALK ABOUT IT ANYMORE!

I CAN'T CONCENTRATE. YOU'RE TURNING ME ON.

I'M GOING TO TAKE YOU WHILE YOU READ.

ALICE! ALICE!

BOM BOM

LOOK AT THESE BOOTS! MY BUDDY SID GAVE 'EM TO ME.

LOOK! WITH MY MUSTACHE AND MY BOOTS, I LOOK LIKE A MUSKETEER!

EN GARDE!

I WENT TO SID'S SHOP TO DRAW THEM. HE LIKED MY DRAWING SO MUCH THAT HE KEPT IT IN EXCHANGE FOR SOME BOOTS. OF COURSE, THEY'RE NOT NEW, BUT NOW I CAN DO SOME SELF-PORTRAITS AS A MUSKETEER.

ALICE? WHY ARE YOU LOOKING AT ME LIKE THAT?

ISAAC, WHAT'S THIS?

UH WELL, IT'S A STUDY PREP-PING FOR A LARGE COMPOSI-TION. IT'S A PORTRAIT OF A MAN IN A MILITARY OUTFIT ON THE DECK OF A SHIP, AGAINST A NAVAL BATTLE SCENE.

YOU'RE NOT THE ONE WHO PAINTED, ARE YOU?

NO, IT'S BY DUFFY.

HOW MUCH DID YOU PAY FOR IT?

I DIDN'T...

YOU GOT IT IN EXCHANGE FOR ONE OF YOUR DRAWINGS, I SUPPOSE.

NO...

I GOT IT PLAYING BACKGAMMON.

YOU DON'T EVEN KNOW HOW TO PLAY CHECKERS! HOW MUCH DID YOU PAY FOR IT?

ARE YOU NOSING ABOUT MY THINGS?

YOUR MESS NEARLY KNOCKED ME OUT WHEN IT FELL OVER. I FOUND IT WHEN I WAS PICKING UP YOUR CANVASES. YOU'D HIDDEN IT!

BAF

JOHN SOLD IT TO YOU!

I NEED THAT PAINTING.

HOW MUCH DID YOU PAY FOR IT?

UH... A HUNDRED.

THREE HUNDRED!

A HUNDRED FIFTY.

THREE HUNDRED!

TWO HUNDRED.

THREE HUNDRED!

ISAAC? DID YOU PAY HIM MORE THAN THREE HUNDRED?

FOUR HUNDRED AND FIFTY.

WHERE DID YOU FIND THE MONEY? DID YOU GO INTO DEBT?

A LITTLE. I SOLD A BUNCH OF DRAWINGS. I DID PORTRAITS OF SHOPKEEPERS.

ISAAC, WE'VE BEEN BARELY GETTING BY FOR WEEKS. MR. BOWLE STILL HASN'T PAID ME. I WORK LATE INTO THE NIGHT, AND YOU HIDE MONEY FROM ME TO BUY THAT LITTLE PIECE OF JUNK FOR YOURSELF!

IT'S BY DUFFY, ALICE!

HOW LONG DID IT TAKE YOU TO AMASS THAT SECRET FORTUNE?

I DON'T KNOW... THREE MONTHS... FOUR MAYBE. ALICE, I NEED THAT STUDY. DUFFY DIED BEFORE HE WAS ABLE TO BEGIN THE PAINTING HE WANTED TO DO FROM IT. I'M GOING TO PAINT SOME LARGE NAVAL SERIES.

THEY'LL CREATE A SENSATION, I'LL EARN THREE OR FOUR TIMES AS MUCH! I WANT TO PAINT SAILORS, BOATS. WE'LL LIVE IN A WEALTHY PORT CITY, FULL OF MERCHANTS, I'LL BECOME AN OFFICIAL PAINTER.

YOU'RE GOING TO RESELL THAT PAINTING!

I CAN'T, ALICE. I WAITED FOR IT, HOPED FOR IT FOR A WHOLE YEAR.

COPY IT AND RESELL IT!

DUFFY IS THE MASTER I MOST ADMIRE.

SHUT UP! SHUT UP!

 CRAC!

 ISAAC?

 IT'S SHIT.

 YOUR SKETCH IS A LOT BETTER. YOU COULD DO A BEAUTIFUL PAINTING FROM THAT.

IN ANY EVENT, NOBODY WILL AGREE TO BUY IT BACK FROM ME AT THE BEAUX ARTS.

 ISAAC, MR. BOWLE HASN'T GIVEN ME ANY WORK IN FOUR DAYS. HE'S GOT MONEY PROBLEMS, TOO.

 ISAAC, YOU NO LONGER NEED THIS PAINTING. YOU CAN DO IT ALL ON YOUR OWN. IF YOU WANT, I'LL BE THE ONE TO GO RESELL IT.

 no!

 I'LL GO MYSELF AND NOBODY WILL WANT IT! WHY DON'T YOU BELIEVE ME? WHY ARE YOU ALWAYS TELLING ME WHAT I'VE GOT TO DO? LIKE I WAS A CHILD!

 I CAN'T WORK, I CAN'T HAVE ANY MONEY, I CAN'T BEHAVE LIKE AN ADULT! I ACT LIKE A BABY! THAT'S WHAT YOU THINK, ISN'T IT?

 SLAM!

YOUNG MAN! YOUNG MAN!

?

EXCUSE ME, YOUNG MAN. I SAW THAT YOU WERE TRYING, UNSUCCESSFULLY, TO SELL THAT LITTLE PAINTING. DO YOU STILL INTEND TO?

MAY I SEE IT?

WOULD YOU LIKE TO BUY IT?

NOT EXACTLY. YOU'RE THE ONE WHO PAINTED IT, RIGHT?

UH... YES.

YOU'RE PRETTY TALENTED, MY FRIEND. WHY DID-N'T YOU SIGN IT?

IT'S JUST A PREPARATORY STUDY. I WANTED TO PAINT A LARGE COMPOSITION.

WHERE DID YOU MEET THE PERSON PORTRAYED?

HE'S... WELL... A PERSON THAT I IMAGINED... THAT IS, COMPOSED AFTER SEVERAL SKETCHES.

IT'S STRIKING. YOU SEEM LIKE YOU KNOW WHAT YOU'RE DOING WITH NAVAL BATTLES. WITHOUT MEANING TO FLAT-TER YOU OVERMUCH, YOUR PAINTING MAKES ME THINK OF DUFFY. YOU MUST KNOW HIM.

I DIDN'T INTRODUCE MYSELF. HENRY DEMELIN, SURGEON.

ISAAC SOPER, PAINTER.

YOU LIKE DUFFY?

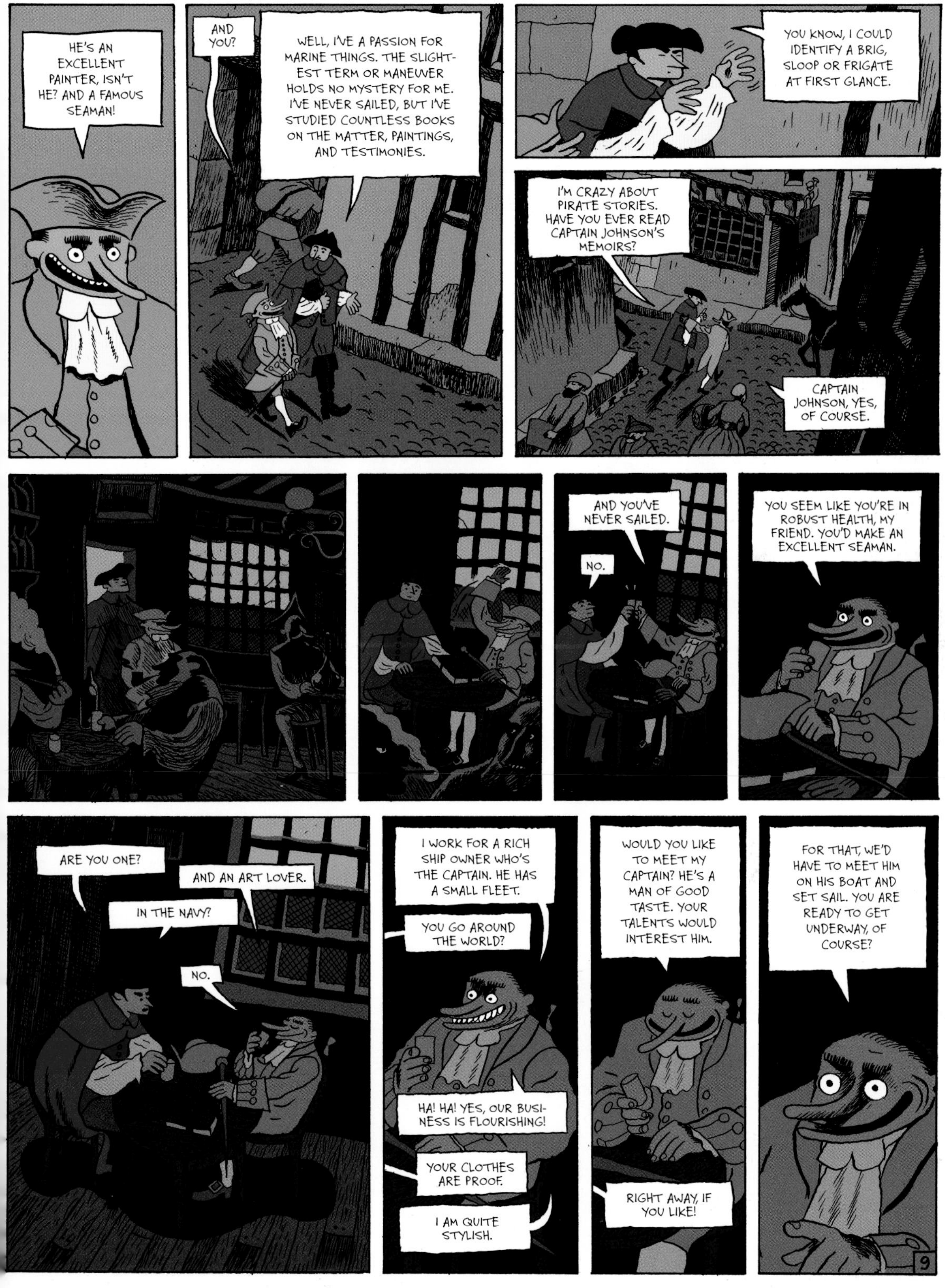
HE'S AN EXCELLENT PAINTER, ISN'T HE? AND A FAMOUS SEAMAN!
AND YOU?
WELL, I'VE A PASSION FOR MARINE THINGS. THE SLIGHTEST TERM OR MANEUVER HOLDS NO MYSTERY FOR ME. I'VE NEVER SAILED, BUT I'VE STUDIED COUNTLESS BOOKS ON THE MATTER, PAINTINGS, AND TESTIMONIES.
YOU KNOW, I COULD IDENTIFY A BRIG, SLOOP OR FRIGATE AT FIRST GLANCE.
I'M CRAZY ABOUT PIRATE STORIES. HAVE YOU EVER READ CAPTAIN JOHNSON'S MEMOIRS?
CAPTAIN JOHNSON, YES, OF COURSE.
AND YOU'VE NEVER SAILED.
NO.
YOU SEEM LIKE YOU'RE IN ROBUST HEALTH, MY FRIEND. YOU'D MAKE AN EXCELLENT SEAMAN.
ARE YOU ONE?
AND AN ART LOVER.
IN THE NAVY?
NO.
I WORK FOR A RICH SHIP OWNER WHO'S THE CAPTAIN. HE HAS A SMALL FLEET.
YOU GO AROUND THE WORLD?
HA! HA! YES, OUR BUSINESS IS FLOURISHING!
YOUR CLOTHES ARE PROOF.
I AM QUITE STYLISH.
WOULD YOU LIKE TO MEET MY CAPTAIN? HE'S A MAN OF GOOD TASTE. YOUR TALENTS WOULD INTEREST HIM.
RIGHT AWAY, IF YOU LIKE!
FOR THAT, WE'D HAVE TO MEET HIM ON HIS BOAT AND SET SAIL. YOU ARE READY TO GET UNDERWAY, OF COURSE?
9

I'M GETTING MARRIED. WE'RE HAVING LOTS OF MONEY PROBLEMS. I...I CAN'T LEAVE HER ALONE.

I UNDER-STAND.

THE TRIP WOULD ONLY LAST A FEW DAYS.

THIS WILL EASE YOUR MIND. WHEN YOU RETURN, SHE'LL MARRY A RICH MAN.

GIVE ME YOUR ADDRESS. I'LL COME BY COACH AND PICK YOU UP AT NINE O'CLOCK. BRING ONLY YOUR ESSENTIALS. YOUR COMFORT ON BOARD WILL BE ASSURED. YOUR WORKING CONDITIONS WILL BE THAT OF A MASTER.

GO BACK HOME NOW. REASSURE HER, BE THE BEST OF MEN. YOU'LL NEVER REGRET THIS DEPARTURE. DON'T GO BRAGGING TO ANY OF THE FELLOW ARTISTS YOU MIGHT MEET, SPEAK ONLY TO HER. SEE YOU SOON, MY FRIEND.

JUMP IN! JUMP IN, MY FRIEND!

WE'RE ALONE?

OF COURSE! TRAVELING IN CARRIAGES IS PAINFUL ENOUGH. MIGHT AS WELL BE COMFORTABLE!

HAVE YOU HAD SUPPER? I'VE SOME FRUIT, SMOKED MEAT, AND BREAD. WE WON'T STOP MUCH DURING THE TRIP.

I'M NOT HUNGRY.

YOU'RE WORRIED. HOW DID SHE TAKE THE NEWS?

SHE WASN'T SO SURE ABOUT IT. SHE WAS SAD.

HAVE YOU LOVED HER VERY LONG?

SINCE CHILDHOOD. NEITHER OF US HAS EVER BEEN WITH ANYONE ELSE.

YOU MUST HAVE MADE A PORTRAIT OF HER. WOULD YOU LET ME SEE IT?

SHE'S A VERY BEAUTIFUL WOMAN. YOU'LL SEE HER AGAIN, MY FRIEND. WE'LL ARRIVE IN TWO DAYS. DO YOU WANT SOME TOBACCO?

I SEE YOU'RE ACHING TO DRAW! THAT'S GREAT! JUST GREAT!

HURRY ALONG, MY BOY. I SEE THE CAPTAIN GETTING AGITATED AND YELLING. WE MUST BE LATE.

THAT'S MY EMPLOYER?

GOOD HEAVENS, NO! HE'S JUST A SMALL-MINDED WINDBAG. A BIT OF ADVICE: KEEP AWAY FROM THAT BRUTE!

THAT IDIOT ALMOST LEFT WITHOUT US. A SAILOR'S READYING OUR CABIN.

I INVITE YOU TO REMAIN ON DECK TO OBSERVE THE SETTING OF THE SAILS.

TOO BAD YOU DON'T HAVE MORE TIME TO DRAW THE PORT. I THINK IT'S VERY BEAUTIFUL.

MR. DEMELIN, WHERE ARE WE GOING AFTER ALL? DURING OUR WHOLE TRIP IN THE COACH, YOU AVOIDED MY QUESTIONS WITH TALES OF PIRACY...(EXCITING ONES, AT THAT). I SAW CONTAINERS DESTINED FOR THE AMERICAS ON THE DECK AND...

EXACTLY.

WE'RE GOING TO THE AMERICAS?

NATURALLY! THAT'S WHERE MY CAPTAIN IS!

YOU CAN STILL JUMP OVER TO THE PIER; WE'RE NOT SO FAR AWAY. COME NOW, THINK ABOUT YOUR CHANCE TO LIVE SUCH AN EXPERIENCE.

MY POOR ALICE!

DO YOU LIKE IT?

YOU DON'T DRAW ANYMORE? YOU DID SOME WATERCOLORS DURING THE CROSSING, MAY I SEE THEM? COME, COME! DON'T POUT. STOP BLAMING YOURSELF, MY BOY! ALICE WILL BE PROUD OF YOU. YOU'LL BE HER GREAT EXPLORER.

DO YOU FEEL THAT NICE, HOT BREEZE? WE'RE VERY CLOSE TO THE CARIBBEAN.

DECK AHOY!

UH OH! THAT IMBECILE CAPTAIN IS RUNNING UP. WHAT'S GOING ON? LET'S GO SEE!

PIRATES! PIRATES!

MAY I, CAPTAIN?

YIKES!

GENTLEMEN, I RECOGNIZE THAT FLAG. IT'S JOHN "THE PILLAGER." ABANDON ANY IDEA OF RESISTANCE!

OH MY GOD!

WHAT SHOULD WE DO, MR. DEMELIN?

KEEP CALM.

AH! HENRY! MY GOOD DOCTOR!

MY DEAR JOHN! HOW ARE YOU?

DID YOU HAVE A GOOD TRIP? I MISSED YOU! WHAT DID YOU BRING US?

HERE'S OUR MAN.

AH HA! A HEARTY FELLOW! COME CLOSER! COME ON!

JOHN! PIRATE!

HA HA!

ISAAC SOPER, PAINTER.

OKAY, WORK FIRST. WHAT DO YOU THINK OF THE CREW?

I SAW SOME BRAVE ONES AMONG THEM. YOU COULD ASK THEM TO JOIN US.

THE CAPTAIN IS A CRUEL, LOUD-MOUTHED FOP. HE'S FROM THE NAVY.

GOOD! IT'LL BE A PLEASURE TO MAKE HIM TELL US WHERE HIS BOOTY IS HIDDEN.

TRY TO DO SO AWAY FROM OUR PAINTER. HE CAN STILL BE A LITTLE SENSITIVE!

HA HA! WELCOME! DON'T BE AFRAID!

FREE WILL REIGNS HERE. YOU'RE NOT OBLIGATED TO STICK WITH ME.

TAP!

THERE'LL BE A BOAT FOR THE SAILORS WHO DON'T WANT TO BE PART OF MY CREW.

BUT DON'T FORGET THAT FORTUNE IS AWAITING YOU!

13

GANGWAY!

LOOK UPWARDS, MY BOY.

WELL NOW, YOU LOOK LIKE YOU'RE A SUFFERING SOUL.

LET'S GET SOME AIR. I ADMIT THAT I'M FEELING A LITTLE DOWN.

THE MEN ARE SICK?

A FEW BOOBOOS, A SPOT OF FEVER... NOTHING MUCH.

NO, IT'S THEIR MORALE THAT'S DOWN. DURING MY ABSENCE, THEY LOST A GOOD FELLOW, A LONGSTANDING SHIPMATE.

HIS NAME WAS GUILVINEC, KNOWN AS "SILVERHOOK," STRUCK DOWN BY A TERRIBLE STOMACH AILMENT. HE RAVED FOR A WHOLE WEEK, HIS GUTS AFIRE, RIGHT BEFORE THE EYES AND EARS OF THE HELPLESS CREW. HIS MIND WAS ALREADY GONE WHEN HE DIED.

MY HAND...IT'S GROWING BACK.

HIS AGONY BROUGHT THEIR SPIRITS DOWN. IN ANY CASE, I COULDN'T HAVE SAVED HIM. A BULLET PUTTING HIM AWAY WOULD'VE BEEN KINDER.

IT BOTHERS JOHN. "SILVERHOOK" HAD BEEN HIS SAILOR FOR TEN YEARS. HE BLAMES HIMSELF FOR NOT HAVING THE HEART TO FINISH HIM OFF.

WHAT'S THAT YOU'RE BRINGING US, JOHN?

THIS TRUNK IS YOURS, PAINTER.

HA HA!

ACCORDING TO WHAT I'VE BEEN TOLD, THERE'S EVERYTHING INSIDE AN ARTIST COULD DESIRE: FINE OILS, PIGMENTS, BRUSHES THAT COME FROM PARIS.

I TOOK IT FROM A SHIP IN THE ROYAL NAVY. THE PAINTER TO WHOM IT BELONGED DIDN'T WANT TO FOLLOW ME.

DO MY PORTRAIT!

GO ON, GO ON!

WELL...HMM...FIRST I HAVE TO DO A SKETCH...A STUDY...THEN...

FINE, FINE!

MOVE ALONG, YOU OTHERS! LET HIM DO HIS WORK!

WELL?

LET ME SEE!

IT'S YOU, WITHOUT A DOUBT!

HA! HA! YOUR LOOK, YOUR MUSTACHE. IT'S JUST A SKETCH, BUT IT'S YOU FOR SURE!

YOU, PAINTER, WILL GET YOUR SHARE RIGHT NOW: TWELVE PIECES OF GOLD AND YOU BUY US THE RUM.

JACK RANSOM! TONIGHT YOU GRILL THE PIG THE WAY YOU DO! WE'RE CELE-BRATING A NICE CAPTURE AND HENRY'S RETURN!

YOU'LL FIND YOURSELF A MATE. YOU TWO WILL SHARE ALL YOUR GOODS AND WOMEN. EXCEPT YOUR PAINTING MATERIALS.

TO SILVERHOOK.

TO HENRY!

TO HENRY!

EAT, DRINK, MY BOY!

I KNEW FROM MY VERY FIRST MEETING WITH THIS YOUNG MAN THAT HE WAS MADE FOR GLORY AND ADVENTURE.

HE WAS CARRYING UNDER HIS ARM A SMALL CAN-VAS WORTHY OF A GREAT MASTER. IT SHOWED A BLOODY BOARDING, IN THE CENTER OF WHICH COULD BE SEEN A FEROCIOUS SEAMAN WHO LOOKED STRANGELY LIKE CAPTAIN PEACH!

YOU KNOW CAPTAIN PEACH? IMPOSSIBLE! YOU'RE TOO YOUNG!

JUST FROM STORIES AND A FEW ENGRAVINGS.

HA HA HA! PEACH! SKILL, CRUELTY, COURAGE, AND DEEDS, WHAT A MAN! HE WAS THE GREATEST! THEY SAY THE DEVIL WAS ON HIS SIDE!

YES! YES! IT'S TOLD THAT ONCE, DURING A GAME OF CARDS WITH HIS BEST MEN...

...HE TOOK HIS PISTOL AND FIRED UNDER THE TABLE. HE DESTROYED HIS SECOND OFFICER'S KNEE, WITH NO EXPLANATION, JUST TO SHOW THAT HE WAS PEACH, THE ONLY ONE WHO COULD DO THAT. GULP.

YOU SEE! YOU SEE! HE'S NOT JUST SOME NOVICE.

PEACH! I'D HAVE LIKED TO HAVE MET THE GUY! THE MOST FEARED MAN IN THE CARIBBEAN. AND A FAMOUS SKIRT-CHASER!

PEACH WAS IMPOTENT.

SUCH BEHAVIOR COULD ONLY BE THAT OF AN IMPOTENT MAN! AND ALTHOUGH PEOPLE SAID HE HAD MANY MISTRESSES, NOBODY EVER SAW A ONE.

WITH ONE EXCEPTION.

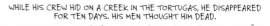

WHILE HIS CREW HID ON A CREEK IN THE TORTUGAS, HE DISAPPEARED FOR TEN DAYS. HIS MEN THOUGHT HIM DEAD.

THEY WERE PREPARING TO SET SAIL WHEN HE REAPPEARED...

...WITH, ON HIS ARM, A VERY YOUNG, SWEET GIRL. THERE WAS NOTHING OF A SLUT ABOUT HER. SHE SEEMED LIKE A VIRGIN. THE MOST SURPRISING THING WAS THAT SHE SEEMED VERY MUCH IN LOVE WITH PEACH AND THAT PEACH HIMSELF LOOKED AS THOUGH HE WERE SMITTEN, FULL OF CONSIDERATION AND TENDERNESS.

HE HAD HER GENTLY BROUGHT ABOARD AND CALLED UPON SIX OF HIS MOST FAITHFUL FOLLOWERS.

HE HAD THEM COME INTO HIS CABIN, WHICH HE DOUBLE-LOCKED. THERE, HE REQUIRED HIS LIEUTENANTS TO EACH TAKE HER AS HE WISHED. THE ACCOMPLICES GREW AFRAID, IMAGINING SOME NEW MACHIAVELLIAN CRUELTY FROM THEIR LEADER. DESPITE THEIR BRUTAL LUST FOR THE OPPOSITE SEX, NARY A ONE DARED TOUCH HER.

THE TERRIFYING PEACH BLACKENED WITH RAGE AND SWORE THEM THE WORST FATE IF THEY DIDN'T CARRY OUT HIS ORDERS.

THE CONDITIONS WEREN'T OPTIMAL FOR THE WRETCHES TO DEMONSTRATE THEIR VIRILITY, BUT THE GIRL HELPED THEM. THEY HAD TO EXERT THEMSELVES IN A THOUSAND FEATS, CONTORTIONS, AND REFINED ABUSES.

IT'S NOT KNOWN HOW MANY TIMES AND HOW MANY DAYS THIS EVENT WAS REPEATED. PEACH BEGAN HIS ADVENTURES ANEW AND THE GIRL DISAPPEARED. SHE WAS NEVER SEEN AGAIN.

IT'S SAID THAT PEACH ENDED UP KILLING HER BECAUSE HE WAS SUFFERING SO FROM NOT BEING ABLE TO DO HER THE HONORS.

THIS TALE IS SO UNUSUAL THAT I'M SURE IT'S TRUE, AT LEAST THE GIST OF IT IS.

AHHH! VERY ASTUTE, YOUNG MAN! YOU'VE SHED A NEW LIGHT ON IT. I AGREE WITH YOUR INTERPRETATION! YES! I LIKE IT!

TO THE PAINTER! HAHAHAHAHAHAHA!

TAP!

TO THE PAINTER! HAHAHAHAHAHAHAHA!

19

GRMB MRRRR

WHO'S THIS WOMAN IN YOUR SKETCHPAD?

UHHH... WELL...SHE'S MY FIANCÉE.

ARE YOU SERIOUS?

UH YEAH, WHY?

YOU'RE KIDDING ME!

HOW COULD YOU GET SUCH A PRETTY WOMAN?

WELL, IT'S TRUE! MOREOVER, IT'S A VERY EXACT PORTRAIT! HER NAME IS ALICE!

I BELIEVE YOU! I BELIEVE YOU! YOU LEFT WITHOUT MARRYING HER!

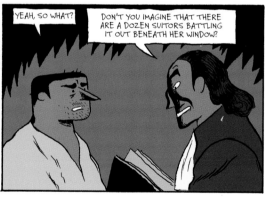

YEAH, SO WHAT?

DON'T YOU IMAGINE THAT THERE ARE A DOZEN SUITORS BATTLING IT OUT BENEATH HER WINDOW?

THEY'RE YOUNG, OLD, MAYBE HANDSOME, SOMETIMES RICH. HALF OF 'EM HAVE ALREADY ASKED FOR HER HAND.

YEAH, WELL IT'S MY FIST THEY'LL GET IN THEIR MOUTH!

HAHAHAHA! I KNOW SOME PRETTY WOMEN, TOO. TONIGHT, I'M GONNA VISIT 'EM BEFORE LEAVING.

BEFORE LEAVING? WHERE ARE WE GOING?

FOLLOW ME.

CHOOSE THE NICEST GET-UP. I WANT YOU TO BE PRESENTABLE. I'M TAKING YOU TO THE GOVERNOR'S HOUSE.

HURRY UP!

HAHAHA! I SEE THAT YOU HAVE GOOD TASTE IN CLOTHES.

GO ON, CLIMB ABOARD. HURRY UP!

HELLO, MY FRIEND!

WE'RE GOING ON THAT BOAT?

IT'S MY BEST CAP-TURE. I'VE REFITTED IT TO MY LIKING. IT'S ALMOST READY.

AND WHERE ARE WE GOING?

FAR FROM THIS ISLE AND THAT CAVE THAT'S DRIVING ME MAD.

AND YOU'LL BOARD SHIPS FROM SUCH A BIG SHIP?

HA HA! WHY? DO YOU LIKE BOARDINGS ALL THAT MUCH?

WE'LL TALK ABOUT IT LATER. FOR NOW, I'M THINKING OF THE BEAUTIES AWAITING US.

WE'LL BE BACK TOMORROW AT NINE. SHORE LEAVE, BOYS! HAVE A GOOD TIME, BUT STAY OUT OF BRAWLS.

BE DISCREET!

I'M VISCOUNT DE BONNEVAL. HIS EXCELLENCY IS EXPECTING US.

FOLLOW ME, PLEASE.

I HAVE TO ATTEND TO SEVERAL MATTERS WITH THE GOVERNOR. TAKE A STROLL IN THE GARDENS, USUALLY THEY'RE WELL FREQUENTED.

HAVE A GOOD DAY, MY BOY.

OH! IF YOU SHOULD MEET THE GOVERNOR'S WIFE, DRAW HER!

LOOK WHAT WE FOUND!

AN ARTIST!

ISAAC, PAINTER.

CAMILLA.

CLOTILDA.

EMILY.

JOSEPHINE.

WHAT DO YOU DRAW, SIR?

WHATEVER I SEE, OR RATHER, WHATEVER I'M TRYING TO UNDERSTAND.

SO YOU LIKE BOTANY.

I'M SUDDENLY MUCH LESS INTERESTED.

BUT I BEG YOU, RESUME YOUR DISCUSSION. FORGET ABOUT ME.

AND YOU'RE GOING TO DRAW US?

NATURALLY. AND I PREFER THAT YOU NOT POSE.

ARE YOU UNDERTAKING A SCIENTIFIC EXPEDITION?

DO YOU KNOW THERE EXISTS PRACTICALLY NO PLEASURE EQUAL TO THAT OF LISTENING TO WOMEN'S CONVERSATIONS?

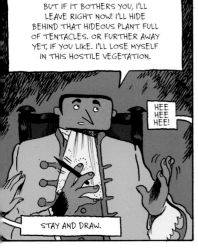

BUT IF IT BOTHERS YOU, I'LL LEAVE RIGHT NOW! I'LL HIDE BEHIND THAT HIDEOUS PLANT FULL OF TENTACLES. OR FURTHER AWAY YET, IF YOU LIKE. I'LL LOSE MYSELF IN THIS HOSTILE VEGETATION.

HEE HEE HEE!

STAY AND DRAW.

WHERE ARE YOU FROM, MONSIEUR PAINTER?

FROM PARIS. A RICH SEAFARER HAD ME COME HERE TO DEPICT HIS ADVENTURES.

FROM PARIS! I'VE NEVER BEEN THERE! AND VERSAILLES? DO YOU KNOW VERSAILLES?

YOU KNOW, I DON'T FREQUENT THE GREAT PEOPLE OF THIS WORLD. I'M BUT A SIMPLE PAINTER.

WHO'S IN DEMAND ALL THE WAY OVER TO THE AMERICAS.

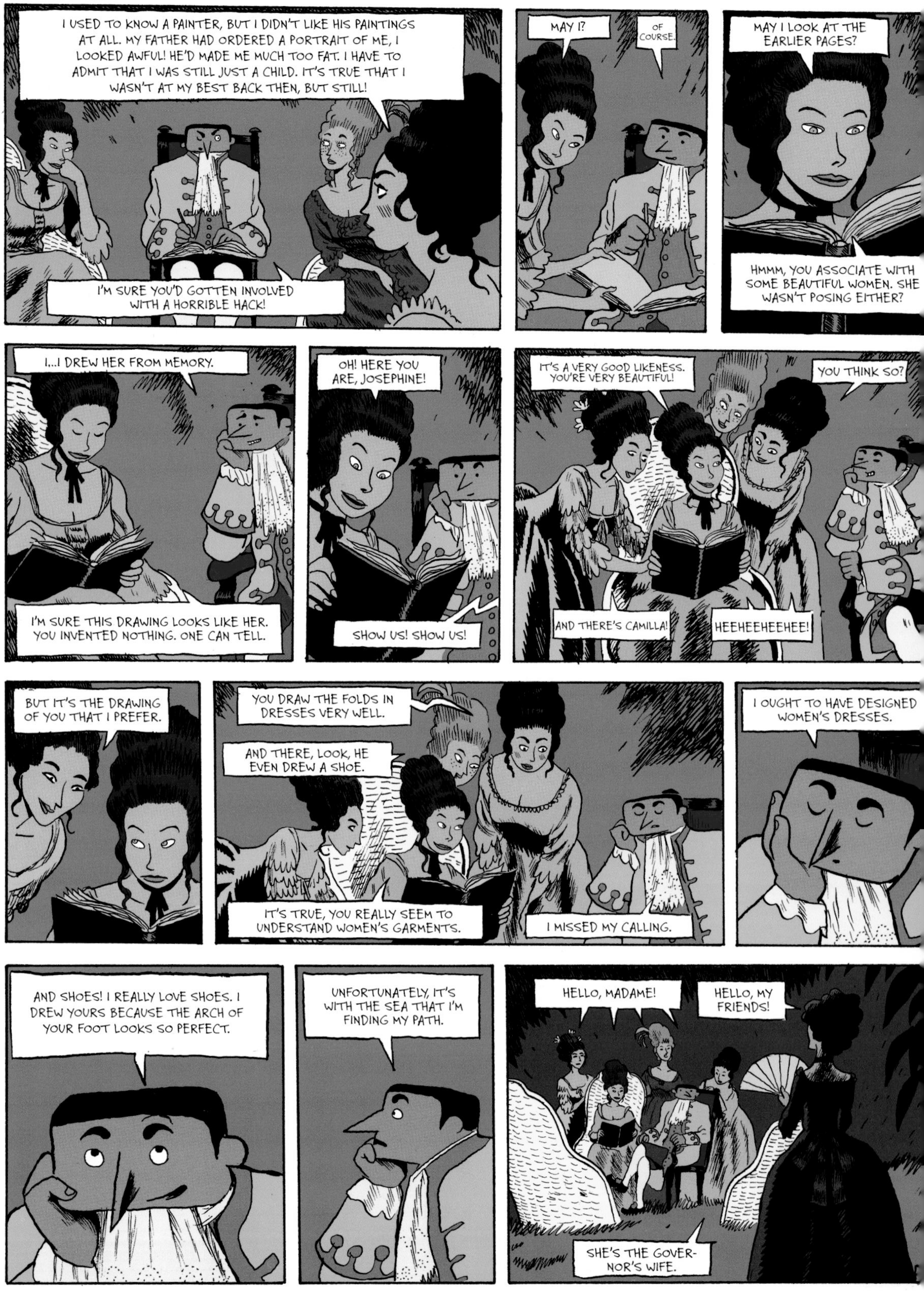
I USED TO KNOW A PAINTER, BUT I DIDN'T LIKE HIS PAINTINGS AT ALL. MY FATHER HAD ORDERED A PORTRAIT OF ME, I LOOKED AWFUL! HE'D MADE ME MUCH TOO FAT. I HAVE TO ADMIT THAT I WAS STILL JUST A CHILD. IT'S TRUE THAT I WASN'T AT MY BEST BACK THEN, BUT STILL!
I'M SURE YOU'D GOTTEN INVOLVED WITH A HORRIBLE HACK!
MAY I?
OF COURSE.
MAY I LOOK AT THE EARLIER PAGES?
HMMM, YOU ASSOCIATE WITH SOME BEAUTIFUL WOMEN. SHE WASN'T POSING EITHER?
I...I DREW HER FROM MEMORY.
I'M SURE THIS DRAWING LOOKS LIKE HER. YOU INVENTED NOTHING. ONE CAN TELL.
OH! HERE YOU ARE, JOSEPHINE!
SHOW US! SHOW US!
IT'S A VERY GOOD LIKENESS. YOU'RE VERY BEAUTIFUL!
YOU THINK SO?
AND THERE'S CAMILLA!
HEEHEEHEEHEE!
BUT IT'S THE DRAWING OF YOU THAT I PREFER.
YOU DRAW THE FOLDS IN DRESSES VERY WELL.
AND THERE, LOOK, HE EVEN DREW A SHOE.
IT'S TRUE, YOU REALLY SEEM TO UNDERSTAND WOMEN'S GARMENTS.
I MISSED MY CALLING.
I OUGHT TO HAVE DESIGNED WOMEN'S DRESSES.
AND SHOES! I REALLY LOVE SHOES. I DREW YOURS BECAUSE THE ARCH OF YOUR FOOT LOOKS SO PERFECT.
UNFORTUNATELY, IT'S WITH THE SEA THAT I'M FINDING MY PATH.
HELLO, MADAME!
HELLO, MY FRIENDS!
SHE'S THE GOVERNOR'S WIFE.

DID YOU KNOW, MADAME, THAT WE'VE FOUND A NEW FRIEND WHO LIKES TO DRAW US?

HE COULD DO YOUR PORTRAIT IN A JIFFY.

IF YOU WISH, MADAME.

HOW AMUSING, I'D HEARD ABOUT YOU.

SHOW ME.

YOU MUST BE VERY DIFFICULT TO DRAW. YOUR FEATURES ARE SO FINE, SO DELICATE!

DON'T FLATTER ME, MY DEAR. OUR FRIEND HAS CERTAINLY MANAGED TO DRAW EACH OF YOU PRETTIER THAN THE OTHERS.

SHOW ME.

BRAVO, SIR. YOU'RE TALENTED.

MY FRIENDS, DON'T FORGET OUR LITTLE GET-TOGETHER IN THE PETIT SALON. MONSIEUR PAINTER, YOU CAN JOIN US IF YOU LIKE. DO AS YOU WISH...

PERHAPS YOU PREFER TO STROLL ABOUT OUR BEAUTIFUL GARDEN.

AND YOU, MISS CLOTILDA, WHERE DO YOU COME FROM?

I'M FROM PARIS, TOO. I ACCOMPANIED MY FATHER WHEN HE GOT AN ADMINISTRATIVE POST HERE.

DO YOU MISS PARIS? WOULDN'T YOU LIKE TO RETURN THERE?

I'M FINE HERE. ISN'T IT RATHER LIKE A PARADISE? MY FATHER HAS INTRODUCED ME TO A CHARMING MAN WHO WORKS WITH HIM. WE'RE ENGAGED. WE'RE GETTING MARRIED NEXT MONTH.

NO, I DON'T WANT TO RETURN TO PARIS.

AND YOU, DO YOU MISS THE BIG CITY? WHAT ARE YOU SEARCHING FOR HERE?

HA HA! ADVENTURE! GOOD FORTUNE!

BY DRAWING YOUNG WOMEN IN GARDENS?

I'D BE HAPPY BEING POOR IF THAT COULD BE MY CAREER.

SO? LET'S SEE YOUR SKETCHPAD!

OH! YES! THAT'S REALLY HER! LOOK, HENRY! THE GOVERNOR'S WIFE!

I WANT YOU TO DO ME A SMALL PAINTING FROM IT, WHICH I'LL HANG IN MY CABIN.

REMEMBER WHEN I WAS TELLING YOU I LOVED BEAUTIFUL WOMEN, TOO? SHE'S MY MISTRESS AND SHE'S EXPECTING ME IN HER ROOM IN A SHORT WHILE.

HA HA! I SEE THAT YOU DIDN'T WASTE YOUR TIME! BEAUTIFUL!

WHICH ONE DID YOU SET YOUR SIGHTS ON?

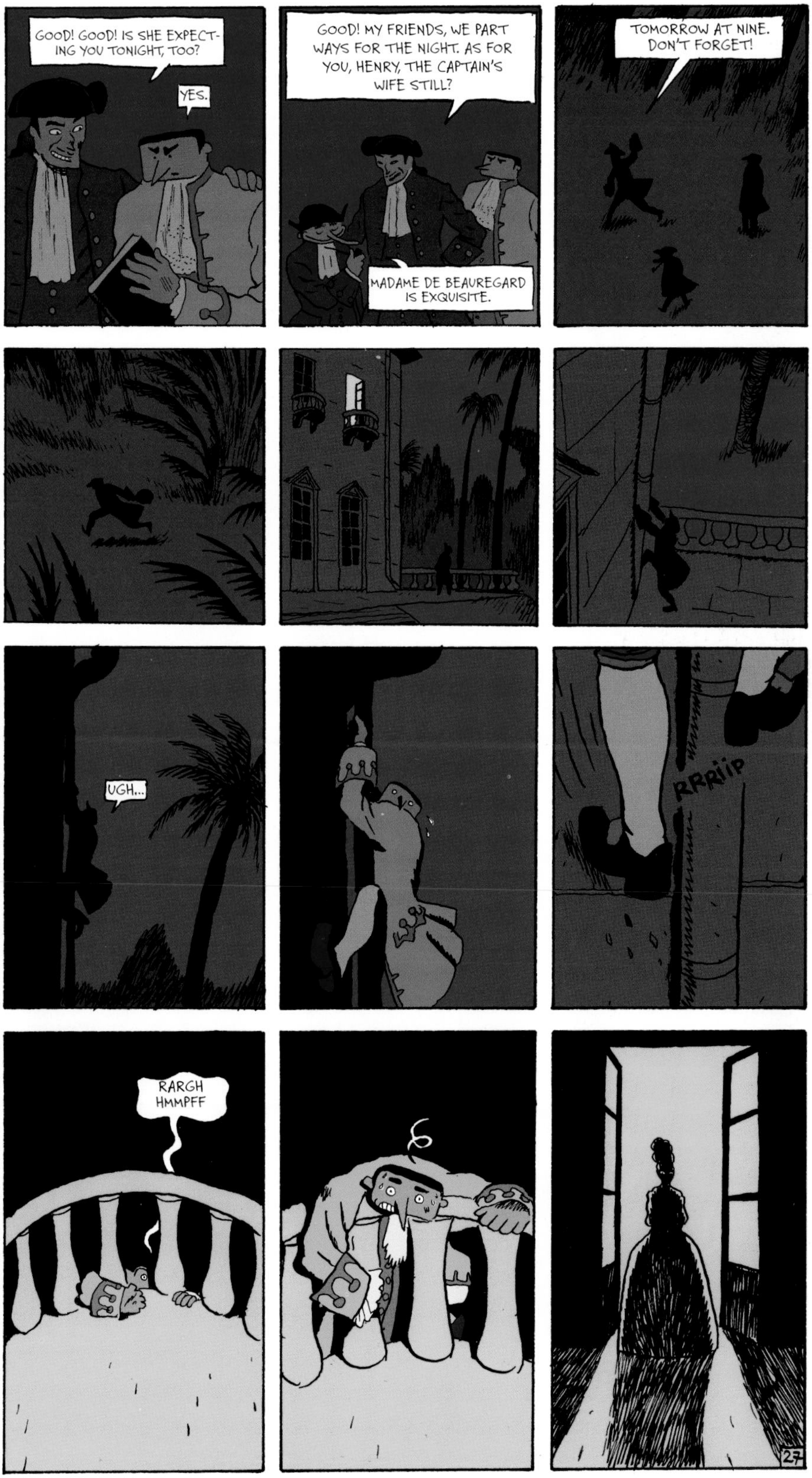
GOOD! GOOD! IS SHE EXPECTING YOU TONIGHT, TOO?
YES.
GOOD! MY FRIENDS, WE PART WAYS FOR THE NIGHT. AS FOR YOU, HENRY, THE CAPTAIN'S WIFE STILL?
MADAME DE BEAUREGARD IS EXQUISITE.
TOMORROW AT NINE. DON'T FORGET!
UGH...
RRRIIP
RARGH HMMPFF

BROOM! BAM!

BALAM!

BLONG!

BLONG

WHAT ARE YOU DOING, MY CHILD?

I'M LEAVING, MONSIEUR TARTON.

WHY'S THAT? DON'T YOU LIKE IT HERE?

I NO LONGER HAVE THE MEANS TO PAY T[...] RENT, MONSIEUR TARTON. I HAVE TO LEA[...]

AAAH, THAT'S WHY YOU'RE CARTING OFF YOUR PAINTER'S THINGS. SPEAKING OF WHICH, JUST WHERE IS HE?

I'VE NOT SEEN HIM IN THREE WEEKS. HAS HE LEFT?

SO HE LEFT, EH? WHY DIDN'T YOU TELL ME SOON-ER? IF YOU CAN'T STAY, COME TO MY PLACE. MY WIFE CAN NO LONGER SEE VERY WELL, AND...

THANK YOU, MONSIEUR TARTON. GOODBYE, MONSIEUR TARTON. GIVE YOUR WIFE A HUG FOR ME.

POOR DEAR, HE LEFT WITHOUT EVEN LEAVING YOU ENOUGH FOR FOOD!

HELLO, MADAME PAILLETTE.

YES, HE DID LEAVE ME SOME MONEY, BUT I'VE HAD NO WORK FOR WEEKS, AND MY MOTHER'S BEEN SICK. THE DOCTORS AND MEDICINES COST VERY DEAR.

HERE'S MY NEW ADDRESS: A LITTLE APARTMENT I FOUND BEYOND THE CITY WALLS. I DON'T KNOW WHEN HE'LL RETURN. GIVE IT TO HIM WHEN HE COMES HERE.

GOODBYE, MADAME PAILLETTE. TAKE GOOD CARE OF YOURSELF.

GOODBYE, MY DEAR YOU KNOW WHERE TO FIND ME IF YOU NEED ME.

PARDON ME, MISS, WHAT ARE YOU SELLING?

NOTHING, SIR. I'M MOVING.

DO YOU PAINT? THOSE ARE CANVASES, AREN'T THEY?

EXCUSE ME, SIR. I HAVE A LONG WAY TO GO TO GET HOME.

WHERE ARE YOU GOING?

TO THE FAUBOURG SAINT-ANDRÉ.

ALLOW ME TO ASSIST YOU. I'M IDLING ABOUT AT A LOOSE END THIS MORNING.

COME ON! LET ME!

PARDON ME, I'M PHILIP DU CHEMIN VERT.

ALICE JEANNENET.

YOU'RE THE NAVIGATOR. I DON'T REALLY KNOW PARIS.

WHERE ARE YOU FROM?

I'M FROM UP NORTH, THE VERY TOP. NEAR MOUNEVILLE. DO YOU KNOW OF IT? IT'S OF NO IMPORTANCE!

I'VE BEEN HERE FOR THREE WEEKS.

BUT IT'S TEMPORARY.

DON'T TELL ANYONE, BUT I'M GOING TO THE INDIES!

REALLY! IT'S TRUE!

29

BUT HONESTLY, IT'S NOT ALL SETTLED. I WANT TO OPEN A COUNTING-HOUSE THERE. I'VE SOLD MY PROPERTY AND HAVE COME IN SEARCH OF INVESTORS HERE.

AND YOU?

I'M FROM HERE.

AND YOU'RE A PAINTER.

MY FIANCÉ IS THE PAINTER.

YOU'RE SELLING HIS PAINTINGS IN THE MARKETS? ARE YOU HIS SALESMAN? HIS AGENT?

NO, SIR! I'M MOVING! MY FIANCÉ LEFT TO BEGIN HIS CAREER AS A NAVAL PAINTER. WHEN HE RETURNS, WE'LL BUY A HOUSE!

YOU NEED MONEY, DON'T YOU?

UH, DO YOU KNOW HOW TO COOK?

YOU SEE, I LOST MY SERVANTS ON THE WAY AND I CAN'T FIND ANYONE TRUSTWORTHY HERE. IF THE JOB INTERESTS YOU, HERE'S MY ADDRESS.

I'LL BE HOME TOMORROW. GOOD DAY, MISS.

3

HELLO! COME IN!

COME ON!

YOU'LL FIND EVERYTHING YOU NEED IN HERE.

UH, OKAY. IT'D BE NICE IF YOU COULD DUST A BIT. HOWEVER, DON'T REORGANIZE, OR I WON'T BE ABLE TO FIND ANYTHING.

MY METHODS FOR ARRANGING THINGS WERE THE PRIME POINT OF CONTENTION BETWEEN ME AND MY GOVERNESS, THE BEST OF WOMEN, BUT WITH A FEROCIOUS DISPOSITION.

IMAGINE AN OLD WOMAN AS TALL AS THAT, WITH A HORRIBLE VOICE LIKE A RATTLE, WHO'D CALL ME "MY BOY," WHO CALLED EVERYONE "MY BOY." WHENEVER YOU'D PASS HER IN THE HALLWAY, THERE WAS ONLY ONE ALTERNATIVE: SHE MADE A FUSS OVER YOU OR THRASHED YOU.

SHE WORKED TO DEATH A COOK AND TWO GROOMS.

YOU MIGHT SAY SHE'S THE ONE WHO RAISED ME AFTER MY MOTHER'S DEATH.

SHE DIDN'T WANT TO COME WITH ME HERE. HER HUSBAND'S IN POOR HEALTH.

I'LL RETURN TO SEE THEM BEFORE MY DEPARTURE. OKAY! I'LL LEAVE YOU, A FRIGHTFUL PILE OF PAPERWORK IS AWAITING ME.

I USUALLY HAVE LUNCH AROUND ONE O'CLOCK OR ONE-THIRTY, BUT TAKE YOUR TIME.

KOF
KOF!

YOU'RE FAMILIAR WITH VAN HEACKEN?

UH, I'D THOUGHT I'D READ ALL HIS WORKS, BUT I'M UNFAMILIAR WITH THIS ONE.

IT'S REMARKABLE, IF A BIT LONG.

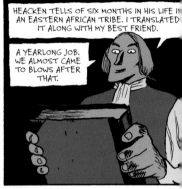

HEACKEN TELLS OF SIX MONTHS IN HIS LIFE I[N] AN EASTERN AFRICAN TRIBE. I TRANSLATED IT ALONG WITH MY BEST FRIEND.

A YEARLONG JOB. WE ALMOST CAME TO BLOWS AFTER THAT.

IT'S YOURS. TAKE IT.

I'M HUNGRY. COULD YOU PREPARE LUNCH?

THEN YOU CAN TELL ME OF YOUR READINGS.

MY FATHER TAUGHT ME TO READ SITTIN[G] ON HIS LAP. HE WAS A MAN OF SCIENCE. [HE] SPOKE SIX LANGUAGES. HE PRACTICED LITTLE MEDICINE AND TAUGHT FOR TE[N] YEARS AT THE UNIVERSITY.

HE HAD TO STOP BECAUSE OF HIS HEART.

MANY OF HIS STUDENTS CONTINUED TO COME TO OUR HOME. WE HAD THOUSANDS OF BOOKS. WE DIDN'T KNOW WHERE TO KEEP THEM ANY LONGER. WE'D MAKE TABLES OUT OF THEM, CHAIRS. PAPA WAS A REAL SIEVE, TOO. WE NO LONGER HAD ENOUGH MONEY TO EAT, YET HE CONTINUED TO BUY BOOKS. WHEN HE PASSED AWAY, MY MOTHER FOUND HERSELF WITH DEBTS AND MY TWO YOUNGER SISTERS TO RAISE. PAPA'S STUDENTS STOPPED HER FROM SELLING THE BOOKS. THEY HELPED US FOR YEARS. SOME OF THEM STILL HELP MAMA FROM TIME TO TIME.

HAVE YOU EATEN? GRAB A PLATE! HAVE A SEAT! HAVE A SEAT!

SO VAN HEACKEN IS YOUR FAVORITE AUTHOR.

I'M FASCINATED HOW EXACT HE IS IN HIS DESCRIPTION OF THE CUSTOMS OF THE PEOPLES THAT HE ENCOUNTERS.

GULP!

IT'S...UH... HMM...GOOD.

GLP.

HE'S THE BEST ETHNOLOGIST IN EXISTENCE, BUT FRANKLY, I FIND HIM TO BE A BIT TEDIOUS.

HIS DUTCH PROTESTANT RIGOR IS STIFLING!

I PREFER DONIEUX TO HIM. ARE YOU FAMILIAR WITH DONIEUX?

AH! YOU'RE GIVING ME A NEW OPPORTUNITY TO ENRICH YOUR LIBRARY.

DONIEUX, TOO, IS A NAVIGATOR. HE'S FULL OF HUMANITY, VIGOR, AND DOUBTS. ON SEVERAL OCCASIONS, HE'S ATTEMPTED TO ESTABLISH COMMUNITIES, TO CREATE UTOPIAS WITH HIS CREWS ON THE COASTS OF FLORIDA AND MADAGASCAR.

IT'S FROM READING HIS LOGS THAT I LEARNED TO NAVIGATE, DESPITE MYSELF. I ENJOY LONG TRIPS, BUT I HATE BOATS. THEY DO A NUMBER ON ME!

DONG DONG

I HAVE TO RUN!

DON'T WORRY ABOUT FIXING SOMETHING TO EAT FOR TONIGHT, I'LL DINE IN TOWN.

UNTIL TOMORROW MORNING!

UH, ALICE! I HAVE A NICE BEDROOM WITH SOME CONNECTING ROOMS IN THE ATTIC. YOU COULD SET UP SHOP THERE. IT WOULD BE MORE PRACTICAL FOR YOUR POSITION. AND YOU COULD READ MY BOOKS.

CONSIDER IT!

HEY! PAINTER! COME ON, OLD BOY! I HAVE TO TALK TO YOU! TODAY'S THE BIG DAY!

SO WHAT'S THIS WITH THE POUTING? I THOUGHT YOU WANTED TO SET OFF FOR ADVENTURES?

33

IT'S YOUR GIRL, UH? IT'S A LOT NICER LEAVING THAN STAYING BEHIND, YOU'LL SEE, HAHAHA! COME ON INSIDE.

YOU'RE GOING TO FIND OUT OUR DESTINATION. SIT DOWN. I WAS WAITING TILL WE'D GOTTEN UNDERWAY TO APPRIZE YOU.

WE'RE SAILING TO THE UTTERMOST SOUTH. DID YOU SEE THE FURS IN THE BETWEEN-DECKS? WE'RE HEADING TOWARDS THE COLDEST CLIMES.

BEYOND THE AMERICAS, WE'LL TRAVERSE A BARRIER OF ICE MOUNTAINS THAT FLOAT ON THE WATER. ON THE OTHER SIDE, THERE'S LAND. I WANT TO BE THE FIRST TO REACH IT.

WE'RE RETRACING THE ROUTE OF MATTHEW BONHOMME.

YOU KNOW OF MATTHEW BONHOMME, MISTER KNOW-IT-ALL?

BONHOMME TOOK THIS ROUTE MORE THAN A HUNDRED YEARS AGO. I FOUND HIS CHARTS AND HIS LOG AT A WINE MERCHANT'S IN SAINT-MALO, ONE OF HIS DESCENDANTS. THE OLD BUGGER PLACED NO VALUES IN THESE RELICS. HE SOLD THEM TO ME AT A DERISORY PRICE.

BONHOMME INTUITED THE PRESENCE OF AN UNKNOWN LAND WHILE ATTEMPTING TO CIRCUMNAVIGATE THE AMERICAS TO THE SOUTH. HIS PROGRESS WAS STOPPED ONCE THE OCEAN BEGAN TO FREEZE. THE ICE WAS SURROUNDING HIS BOAT.

HE HAD TO TURN BACK, BUT HE HAD THE OPPORTUNITY TO SEE THE COASTS OF A NEW WORLD. HE SAW LIFE THERE, BUT WAS UNABLE TO SEE WHETHER THEY WERE MEN OR CREATURES OF A NEW KIND.

HE SAW MANY UNKNOWN ANIMALS. IT'S CERTAIN THESE LANDS HOLD GREAT RICHES.

NOBODY GAVE CREDENCE TO HIS TALE UPON HIS RETURN. HE WAS UNABLE TO FIND FUNDS TO UNDERTAKE A SECOND EXPEDITION. HE DIED FORGOTTEN SHORTLY THEREAFTER.

I'M FOLLOWING HIS ROUTE. YOU'RE GOING TO TAKE BACK IMAGES OF THIS NEW WORLD AND PEOPLE WILL BELIEVE ME. THIS LAND WILL BEAR MY NAME. I'VE BEEN PREPARING FOR THIS ADVENTURE FOR THREE YEARS.

WHEN WILL WE BE BACK?

YOU'RE GOING DOWN IN HISTORY!

WITH A FEW WEEKS OUT OF YOUR LIFE, YOU'LL BECOME THE KING OF THE WORLD!

DIDN'T YOU WRITE YOUR FIANCÉE A LETTER BEFORE LEAVING? THEN, SHE WON'T WORRY AND SHE'LL WAIT FOR YOU!

ARE YOU DISAPPOINTED? DO YOU REGRET BEING A PIRATE? YOU'RE CRAZY! YOU HAVE NO IDEA WHAT BEING A PIRATE'S LIKE. PEACH MARKED PIRACY WITH HIS NAME, BUT I'LL DO BETTER THAN HIM!

CAN YOU COMPARE SUCH GLORY TO THAT OF SKULKING ABOUT SOME STINKING CAVE?

BONHOMME MADE IT THERE WITH RUDIMENTARY NAVIGATIONAL SKILLS AND A WALNUT HULL. I HAVE A MODERN SHIP AND, COMPARED TO HIM, UNMATCHED KNOWLEDGE. WE'RE ALMOST THERE!

FROM NOW ON, YOU'LL PAINT EVERY DAY!

DON'T ASK ANYMORE QUESTIONS. DON'T DISAPPOINT ME! JACK RANSOM WILL FASTEN YOUR EASEL TO THE DECK. YOU'LL BE ABLE TO PAINT EVEN DURING A TEMPEST. GO ON! GET TO WORK!

THAT'S ENOUGH POSING, BARREL-BELLY! IT'S MY TURN! HEY LOOK, PAINTER, I'LL SHOW YOU SOMETHING.

LOOK HOW A PIRATE FIGHTS!

MOVE OVER A LITTLE, RASCAL. I'LL POSE WITH YOU; IT'LL BE LIKE A DUEL!

OH YEAH! THAT'S GREAT!

CHA!

CHA!

HEY! RASCAL! MY PICTURE'S NOT DONE!

35

COME DOWN FROM THERE, RASCAL, SO THE PAINTER CAN FINISH!

YOU'RE KEEPING THE PAINTER FROM WORKING, BARREL-BELLY!

SHUT UP, POWDER-KEG!

THAT'S A STRANGE PICTURE, BUT I DO RECOGNIZE RASCAL. WILL YOU DO A FINISHED PAINTING FROM THAT?

YOU SEE? YOU CAN SEE GOOD HOW HE SLUGS BARREL-BELLY!

DO YOU THINK THEY'LL KNOW HOW TO BEHAVE AS DISCOVER-ERS OF A NEW WORLD?

LOOK AT WHAT THE PAINTER'S DONE, RASCAL!

YOU COME OVER HERE!

OHH, BARREL-BELLY, LOOK!

WELL, DAMN!

JOHN! JOHN! ON THE PORTSIDE.

I'VE BEEN WATCHING 'EM FOR SOME TIME NOW; THEY'RE FOLLOWING US. DO YOU THINK THEY'D DARE ATTACK US?

THEY LOOK LIKE IT. THEY'VE GOT GUTS. WE'RE ALREADY PRETTY FAR FROM THE COAST!

JOHN, I KNOW WE'RE NO LONGER PIRATES, BUT RAISE YOUR FLAG. MAYBE THEY WON'T DARE ATTACK US.

WHO COULD IT BE? EDWARDS? OR THE STAMMERER? ON THE CON-TRARY, MY FLAG MIGHT WELL MOTIVATE THEM.

INCREASE OUR SPEED! I DON'T WANT THEM TO SINK THE BOAT!

THERE'S TWO OF THEM NOW. ONE OF 'EM IS EDWARDS. I RECOGNIZE HIM ON THE BRIDGE!

THEY'RE FASTER! THEY'RE GONNA ATTACK US ON BOTH SIDES!

WE CAN'T AVOID BATTLE.

THAT WAS TO BE EXPECTED.

I DON'T KNOW THE OTHER ONE. I'M SURE EDWARDS KNOWS HE'S DEALING WITH ME. WE WERE BETRAYED OR SPIED UPON.

THAT LIMPDICK TEAMED UP WITH SOME LOWLIFE TO ATTACK ME.

YOU WANTED TO SEE A BOARDING? YOU WANT TO KNOW WHAT PIRACY'S LIKE?

TO ARMS! TO ARMS!

BROM BROM

HE'S STAYING OUT OF RANGE!

OF COURSE!

THE OTHER ONE'S GONE AHEAD. HE'S BLOCKING OUR PATH.

ARRH! EDWARDS IS ALREADY BEHIND US! IF ONLY WE WERE LIGHTER! THAT BASTARD HAS ALWAYS MANEUVERED WELL! BUT WE'RE BETTER THAN HIM AT HAND-TO-HAND! DOES HE WANT TO BOARD? LET HIM! TOO BAD FOR HIM!

POW, BOOM, POW

DON'T STAY THERE! GO INTO THE CHART-ROOM! UNDER THE TABLE, WITH TWO LOADED PISTOLS.

37

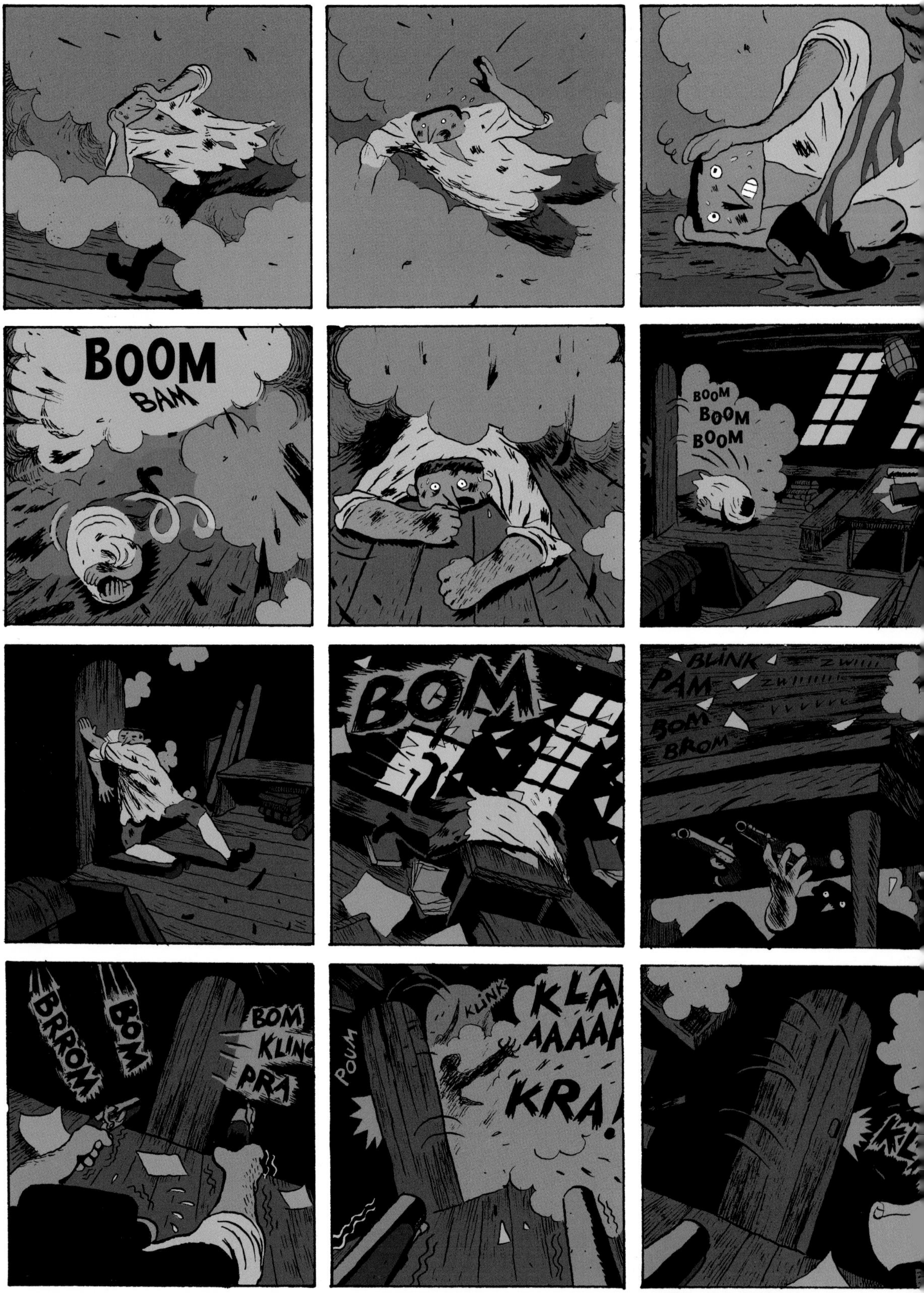
BOOM
BAM
BOOM
BOOM
BOOM
BOM
BLINK
PAM
BOM
BROM
BRROM
BOM
BOM
KLIN
PRA
POUM
KLINK
KLA
AAAA
KRA!
KL

DON'T SHOOT! DON'T SHOOT! IT'S ME JOHN!

PAINTER? YOU IN THERE? YOU'RE NOT WOUNDED?

ANSWER ME! I'M COMING IN, PROMISE YOU WON'T SHOOT!

YES, NO...

LOUDER!

COME IN!

ARE YOU OKAY, MY BOY?

DON'T COME OUT NOW! IT'S OVER. I'LL TELL YOU WHEN YOU CAN. AND LAY DOWN THOSE PISTOLS! YOU'RE SCARING ME LIKE THAT.

JOHN! JOHN! EDWARDS IS DEAD!

AS FOR THE REMAINING ONES, RASCAL SAYS WE SHOULD HANG 'EM FROM THE YARDARMS OF THEIR SHIPS AND LEAVE 'EM TO DRIFT.

NO, WE DON'T MAS- SACRE ANYONE.

JOHN! WE HAVE TO SET AN EXAMPLE! THEY CAN'T JUST GET AWAY LIKE THAT!

EDWARDS IS ENOUGH!

LISTEN...

NO MASSACRES.

DO YOU WANT TO APPEAR AN IMPOTENT?

!?

EXCUSE ME! HUH?...ALICE!

ALICE? WHAT ARE YOU DOING HERE?

UH WELL, I'M ALL DONE, SIR. SINCE YOU NEVER EAT AT HOME THERE'S NOTHING MORE TO DO.

OKAY! VERY GOOD! I WAS JUST THINK-ING OF YOU. COME BACK WITH ME!

I DIDN'T KNOW YOU WERE COMING BACK. IF YOU WANT, I'LL GO BUY SOMETHING TO FIX FOR YOU TO EAT.

SURELY NOT!

COME, COME! GO ON! NO QUESTIONS.

UH, I DIDN'T CLEAN THE OFFICE BECAUSE I DIDN'T KNOW IF...

I DON'T CARE!

I'M OVERWHELMED! THE PAPERWORK, THE LETTERS, THE ACCOUNTS, BUSINESS MEETINGS, CARDS!

I'M AN ADVEN-TURER, EXPLOR-ER, MERCHANT, IF YOU LIKE, BUT NOT SOME PAPER-PUSHER!

DIDN'T YOU WORK FOR A NOTARY PUBLIC? YOU CAN READ AND WRITE. SO HELP ME THEN.

LAY ASIDE YOUR DUST RAGS; THAT'S OVER!

I'VE ALREADY FOUND SOMEONE TO REPLACE YOU.

RIGHT. YOUR WAGES ARE TRIPLED. I'M NOT DOING YOU A FAVOR; IT'LL BE A DIFFICULT TASK.

I NEED YOU FULL TIME. YOU'LL USE THE OFFICE AND THREE ROOMS ON THE THIRD FLOOR. MAKE THEM INTO YOUR LIVING AREA.

SET YOUR OWN SCHEDULE, YOU'LL HARDLY EVER SEE ME.

YOU'LL USE THE ATTIC TO STORE YOUR PAINTER'S THINGS.

I'VE HIRED SOME STRONG BACKS TO DO THE MOVE. THIS AFTERNOON, IF YOU LIKE.

I NEED YOU HERE. SO? IS IT YES? IF YOU REFUSE, I'M FIRING YOU BECAUSE YOU'RE A HORRIBLE COOK! YOUR STEW IS LIKE POISON! REALLY AWFUL!

I ALMOST THOUGHT YOU WERE TRYING TO KILL ME WITH IT!

44

HEY! CAREFUL, YOU LOUTS!

WHAT YOU'RE CARRYING THERE IS AWFULLY FRAGILE!

SET IT THERE.

MAY I SEE THEM ONE DAY, ALICE?

OF COURSE.

I MIGHT EVEN BUY ONE IF I LIKE IT. NATURALLY, I'LL AWAIT YOUR PAINTER'S RETURN.

NOW YOU'LL HAVE MORE ROOM.

ARE YOU SURE YOU DON'T WANT TO MOVE HERE?...

YOU'RE RIGHT. YOU'LL WORK THAT MUCH BETTER.

THAT MUSIC MAKES ME WANT TO DANCE.

I AGREE WITH YOU. THE GREAT REGRET OF MY LIFE IS NOT HAVING GONE OFTEN ENOUGH TO SALONS AND COURTS TO BE A GOOD DANCER.

WE'RE NOT AT THE COURT, SO DANCE!

I WOULDN'T DARE MAKE A SPECTACLE OF MYSELF.

ADMIT, RATHER, THAT YOU'D BE ASHAMED TO BE SEEN WITH A LITTLE COMMONER.

YOU ASKED FOR IT! I'M A DEPLORABLE DANCER!

I'M STEPPING ON YOUR FEET AND I DON'T KNOW HOW TO LEAD YOU.

THEN I'LL LEAD YOU.

I'VE NEVER FELT SO CLUMSY, BUT IT'S NICE.

NOBODY'S EVER TRIED TO TEACH YOU?

CLAP CLAP CLAP

OKAY...UH...I HAVE TO GET HOME.

ALL RIGHT! GO ON HOME! HURRY OFF TO BED! DON'T FORGET THAT WE BEGIN TOMORROW AT DAWN!

STAY LYING DOWN, SHARKEY. HENRY SAID YOU SHOULDN'T MOVE.

I WANT TO STAND TO SEE YOU OFF, JOHN.

AND YOU, ONE-EYE, YOU POOR FELLOW.

I WANNA GO WITH YOU, JOHN. I'LL BE BACK ON MY FEET IN A WEEK!

46

YOU WOULDN'T LAST TWO WEEKS ON THE OCEANS, BOYS.

I'LL WATCH OVER 'EM, JOHN.

YOU'LL GET YOUR SHARE ALONG WITH THE REST OF US WHEN I RETURN.

RASCAL'S THE ONE WHO WANT-ED US TO BURY THEM LIKE THAT.

?

WHAT'S WITH THEM AND THEIR BIBLES? RASCAL IS BRAVE.

BUT I HATE HIM WHEN I SEE HIM PRAYING AND BOWING. HE ACTS LIKE SOME OLD WOMAN.

AND YOU, PAINTER, DO YOU BELIEVE WHAT'S WRITTEN IN THAT BIBLE?

I'M AN ATHEIST. WELL, I'M A JEW, BUT AN ATHEIST NONETHELESS.

ARE YOU AN UNBELIEVER, YES OR NO?

YES.

THAT'S FINE! YOU'RE A REAL PIRATE.

SOME PIRATES BELIEVE IN GOD.

YES, BUT NOT ME! I BELIEVE IN MYSELF, IN MY BOAT, IN MY CREW, IN YOU, IF YOU'RE TRUSTWORTHY!

I CAN'T STOP THEIR GARBAGE ON BOARD, BUT THEY AGGRAVATE ME!

LOOK AT HENRY! HE SAVED ONE-EYE AND SHARKEY WITH HIS HANDS AND HIS SKILL, NOT BY PRAYING TO I DON'T KNOW WHAT!

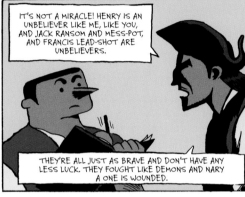

IT'S NOT A MIRACLE! HENRY IS AN UNBELIEVER LIKE ME, LIKE YOU, AND JACK RANSOM AND MESS-POT, AND FRANCIS LEAD-SHOT ARE UNBELIEVERS.

THEY'RE ALL JUST AS BRAVE AND DON'T HAVE ANY LESS LUCK. THEY FOUGHT LIKE DEMONS AND NARY A ONE IS WOUNDED.

I'VE WATCHED THEM. MAYBE THEY'RE UNBELIEVERS, BUT THEY DON'T LIKE THE IDEA THAT THE DEAD DON'T GO SOMEWHERE.

JACK RANSOM! DID YOU KNOW THE DEAD DON'T GO ANYWHERE?

WHAT DID YOU SAY, JOHN?

HOW FAR ALONG ARE YOU?

I'VE ALMOST FINISHED. IF ALL GOES WELL, WE'LL SET SAIL THIS AFTERNOON.

HEY, PAINTER! DID YOU DRAW ME WHEN I WAS HANGING ON THE YARDARM?

YOU'LL SHOW ME WHAT YOU DID, OKAY?

I PROMISE, JACK.

YOU ALWAYS DRAW, PAINTER, WHEN DO YOU EVER PAINT?

I NEED DRAWINGS. AFTERWARDS, I'LL DO LARGE COMPOSITIONS FROM THEM.

DO YOU WANT ME TO THROW SOMETHING TOGETHER ON THE TOPSAIL LIKE I DID ON THE DECK? YOU COULD REALLY SEE THE OCEAN LIKE THAT.

UH, YEAH, MAYBE.

OKAY, I'D BETTER GET TO BED IF I WANT TO WORK TOMORROW.

GOOD NIGHT, JOHN. GOOD NIGHT, JACK!

GOOD NIGHT, PAINTER.

JACK, DO YOU THINK THE DEAD GO ANYWHERE?

Christophe Blain

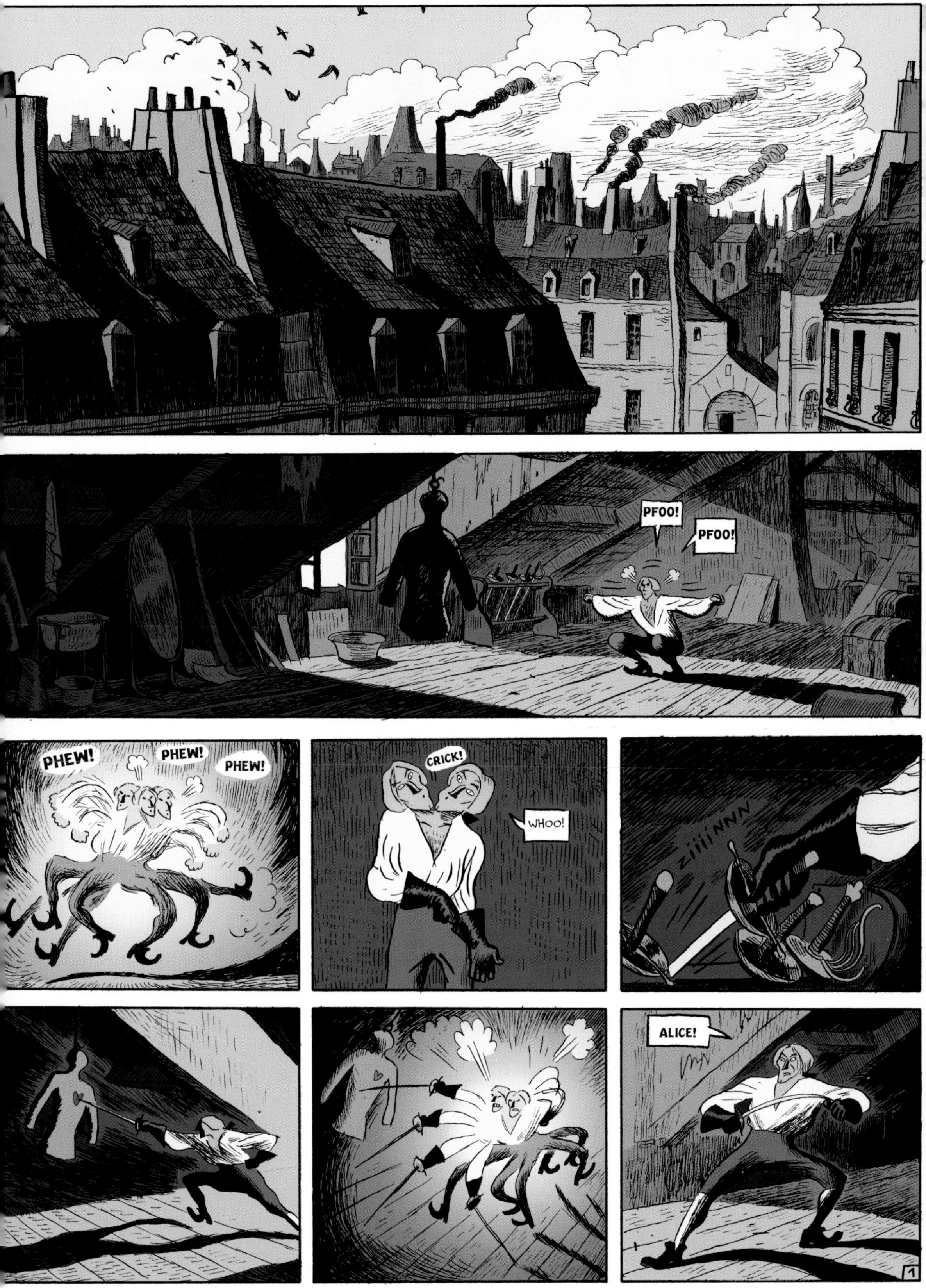
PFOO!
PFOO!
PHEW!
PHEW!
PHEW!
CRICK!
WHOO!
ALICE!

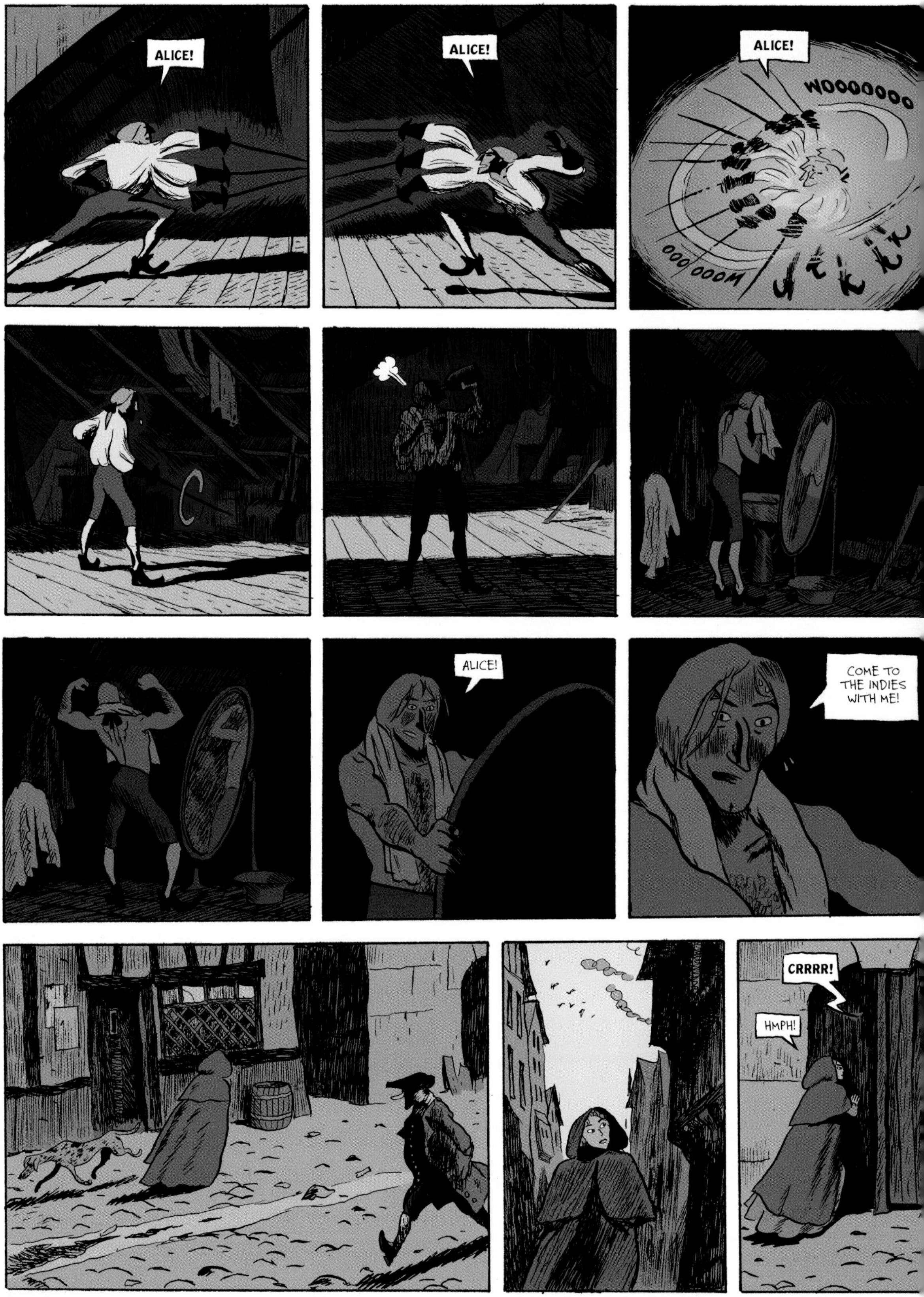
ALICE!
ALICE!
ALICE!
WOOOOOOO
WOOO OOO
ALICE!
COME TO THE INDIES WITH ME!
CRRRR!
HMPH!

AH, MY CHILD! DEAR CHILD! I WAS EXPECTING YOU.

HELLO, MADAME PAILLETTE.

HELLO! HELLO! COME!

THIS WAY!

COME SEE WHAT I HAVE FOR YOU!

I MADE SURE NOBODY OPENED IT, DESPITE ALL THESE PRYING FOLK!

IT ARRIVED THREE DAYS AGO!

WHAT?! WHY DON'T YOU GET A MOVE ON, YOU! SCAT! GET OUT OF HERE! DIRTY PIG!

IT WAS OLD MAN TARTON. WHAT AN OLD SWINE HE IS. AND NOSY, TOO!

SO HE WROTE YOU, EH? WHAT'S HE GOT TO SAY?

THANK YOU, MADAME PAILLETTE. GOODBYE.

SO, YA AIN'T OPENIN' IT?

I'LL COME SEE YOU AGAIN SOON.

OH! SORRY, ALICE!

DID I HURT YOU?

HE WROTE ME! HE SENT SOME DRAWINGS!

LOOK.

HE'S A REMARKABLE ARTIST. WHEN'S HE RETURNING?

SOON, I THINK. SEVERAL WEEKS, PERHAPS, A MONTH OR TWO.

HE MUST BE AT SEA RIGHT THIS VERY MINUTE.

FINE! GO ON BACK HOME.

OH, SHIT! SHIT!

CRRAC!

FLAPFLAPFLAP

SHIT!
SHIT!
SHIT!

WHAT THE HELL YOU DOING HERE?

BORED STIFF.

DRAW!

I'VE ALREADY DRAWN EVERY-THING.

THE BRIDGE, THE PROW, THE TOPSAIL, THE STERN, THE MAIN DECK, THE QUARTERDECK, YOU, THE OTHERS...

I FORBID YOU TO GET BORED. DRAW. WHERE'S YOUR SKETCHPAD?

GO FIND A SKETCHPAD AND DRAW. YOU'LL DRAW EVERY DAY!

CRRRAAAA

RAAA

FFCHH

BRRROOOOO

HELP ME PUT OUT THIS DAMN THING BEFORE IT BUSTS.

CHHR

BRO

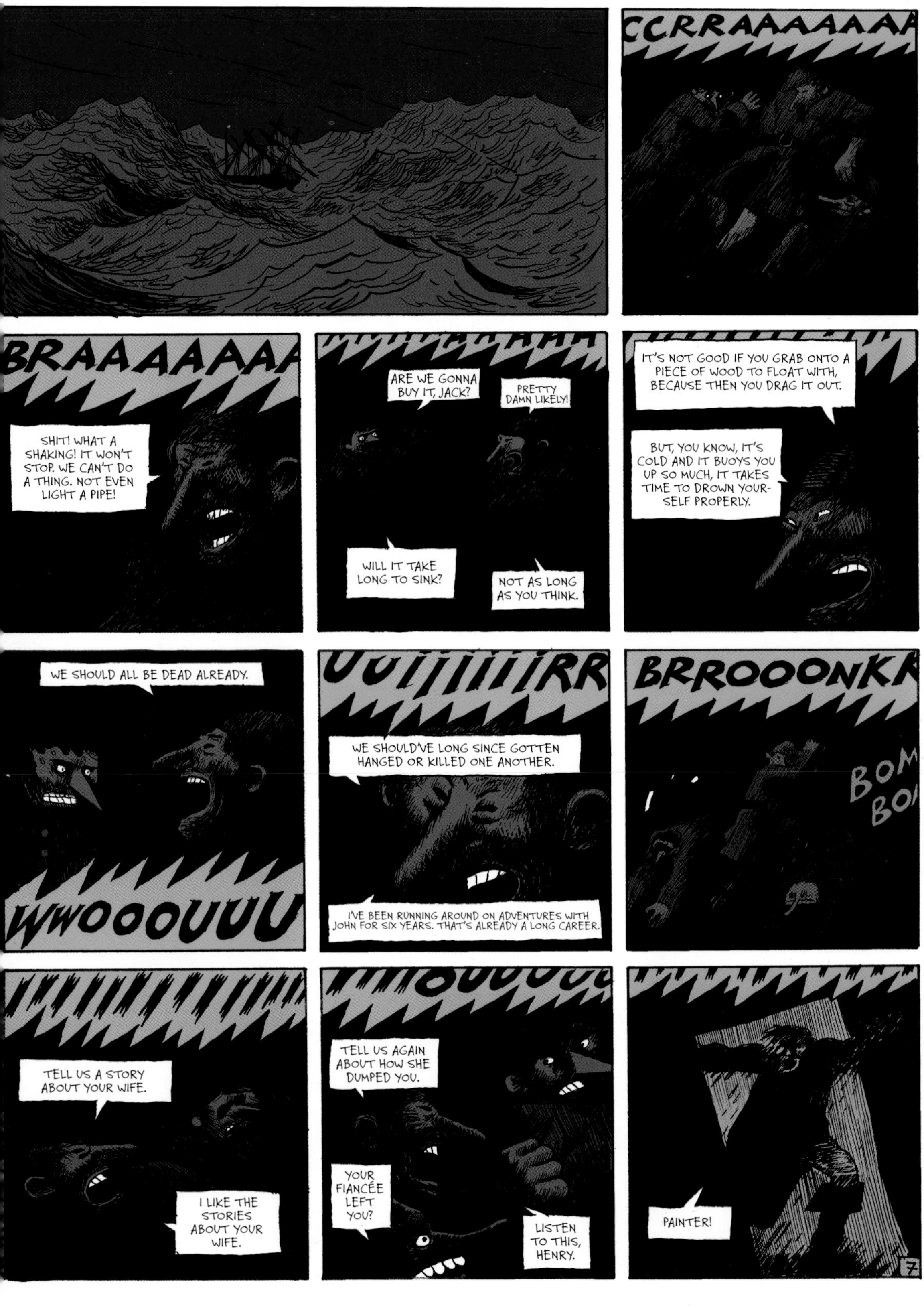
CCRRAAAAAAA
BRAAAAAAA
SHIT! WHAT A SHAKING! IT WON'T STOP. WE CAN'T DO A THING. NOT EVEN LIGHT A PIPE!
ARE WE GONNA BUY IT, JACK?
PRETTY DAMN LIKELY!
WILL IT TAKE LONG TO SINK?
NOT AS LONG AS YOU THINK.
IT'S NOT GOOD IF YOU GRAB ONTO A PIECE OF WOOD TO FLOAT WITH, BECAUSE THEN YOU DRAG IT OUT.
BUT, YOU KNOW, IT'S COLD AND IT BUOYS YOU UP SO MUCH, IT TAKES TIME TO DROWN YOURSELF PROPERLY.
WE SHOULD ALL BE DEAD ALREADY.
WWOOOUUU
UUIIIIIIIRR
WE SHOULD'VE LONG SINCE GOTTEN HANGED OR KILLED ONE ANOTHER.
I'VE BEEN RUNNING AROUND ON ADVENTURES WITH JOHN FOR SIX YEARS. THAT'S ALREADY A LONG CAREER.
BRROOOONKR
BOM
BO
TELL US A STORY ABOUT YOUR WIFE.
I LIKE THE STORIES ABOUT YOUR WIFE.
TELL US AGAIN ABOUT HOW SHE DUMPED YOU.
YOUR FIANCÉE LEFT YOU?
LISTEN TO THIS, HENRY.
PAINTER!

COME LOOK A LITTLE AT WHAT'S GOING ON OUTSIDE!

YOU HAVE TO SEE THIS UP CLOSE. IF WE MAKE IT, YOU'LL HAVE TO REMEMBER IT WELL TO PAINT IT!

JOHN!

I'LL KEEP HIM SAFE WITH A ROPE, HENRY! ANYHOW, THERE'S A CHANCE WE MAY NEVER MAKE IT!

COME FORWARD! COME TO THE FRONT!

GO BACK?

GO BACK!

YOU'RE NUTS!

9

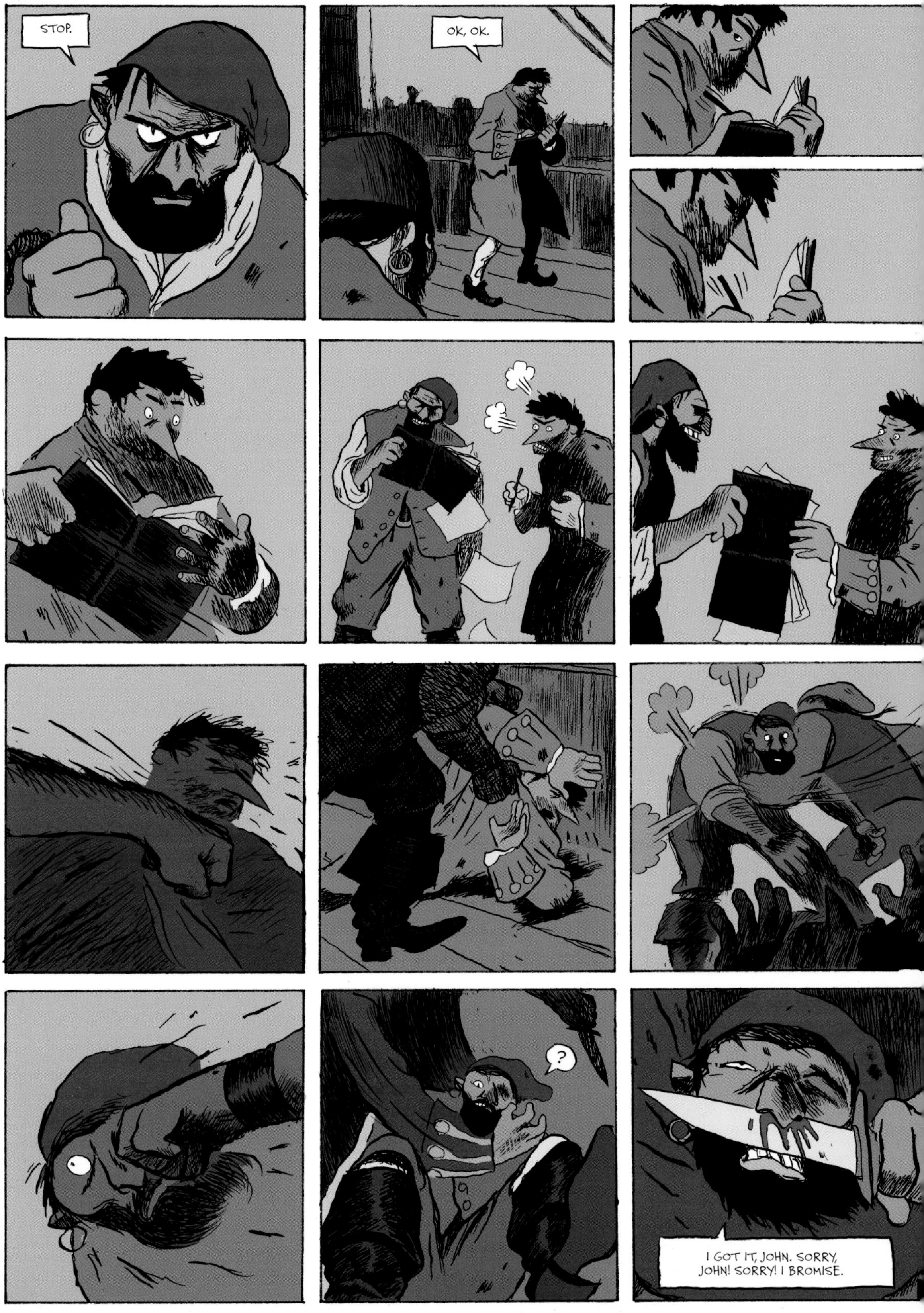
STOP.
OK, OK.
?
I GOT IT, JOHN. SORRY, JOHN! SORRY! I BROMISE.

I'LL DEAL WITH IT, JOHN!

WHY DIDN'T YOU STEP IN SOONER, JOHN?

JUST TO SEE. I THOUGHT THE PAINTER WOULD AVOID IT.

THERE, ALL SEWN UP, MY FRIEND. NOW YOU HAVE A REAL PIRATE'S SCAR THERE. I DON'T KNOW IF YOUR NOSE WILL GO BACK TO ITS ORIGINAL SHAPE.

HOLD THAT A MOMENT. YOU'LL HAVE TO DRAW WITH ONLY ONE EYE FOR A TIME.

I'M TIRED OF THESE BRUTES, HENRY.

IF WE'RE NOT TOO RILED UP THIS EVENING, I'D SUGGEST YOU GATHER UP ALL YOUR DRAWINGS FROM THESE PAST WEEKS AND SHOW THEM TO OUR EXPLORERS. WE'LL THROW IN AN EXTRA RATION OF RUM TO GO ALONG WITH YOUR SHOW.

HAR HAR HAR HAR!

HA HA HA HA HA HA!

LOOK! LOOK AT THAT! THAT'S ME CLIMBING UP THE TOPMAST.

SHOW US! SHOW US!

AND ME? WHERE AM I?

WHO'S THAT?

YOU DRAW TOO BLURRY, PAINTER.

AND THERE, ON THE YARDARM! IT'S ME AGAIN!

YOU SURE?

LOOK AT THE EARS, IDIOT! AIN'T THAT ME?

HEY, HEY NOW! GENTLEMEN! HANDLE THOSE MASTERPIECES WITH CARE!

HEY! THE PAINTER KNOWS HOW TO DRAW WOMEN, TOO!

LOOK AT THAT ONE! SHE'S DONE BETTER!

SHE AIN'T BLURRY.

SHOW ME!

HE PUT HIMSELF MORE INTO IT.

HE WAS TRYING TO FLATTER HER, NO DOUBT.

DID YOU REALLY SEE 'EM?

DID YOU SCREW 'EM?

HE COULDN'T HAVE HAD SUCH PRETTY ONES.

LOOK HOW THEY'RE DRESSED, IT'S SILK.

THOSE ARE RICH WOMEN!

YOU CAN MAKE UP WOMEN WITHOUT LOOKING?

OF COURSE.

THEN I WANT ONE LIKE THAT ONE.

THAT ONE'S HIS WIFE.

OH?

IT'S TRUE.

YOU DIDN'T PRETTY YER WIFE UP A TAD, DID YOU?

HER PORTRAIT IS AS EXACT AS YOURS IN THESE PAGES, LEAD-SHOT.

HENRY MUST BE RIGHT, LEAD-SHOT. THE PAINTER DIDN'T MAKE YOU HAND-SOME AND YOU AIN'T HANDSOME.

HA HA HA HA HA HA HA HA!

WHAT ARE YOU DOING HERE WITH US?

YOU OUGHT TO BE SCREW-ING HER RIGHT NOW.

YOU LET HER GET SCREWED BY OTHER GUYS?

IS SHE DEAD?

WHAT KIND OF WOMAN DO YOU WANT, LEAD-SHOT?

I WANT ONE WITH MORE TITS AND ASS.

FAT?

YEAH!

CRAC

THERE. SHE'S ALL YOURS.

HA HA HA!

HO HO!

A BLOND! DO A BLOND! WITH LOTS OF HAIR.

HEY! PAINTER, DO AN EVEN FATTER ONE!

HA HA HA HA

YOU'RE AN ACE!

SMOKE! SMOKE! IT'S MY BEST TOBACCO!

HOW'S YOUR EYE?

YOU STILL DON'T HAVE A MATE, HMM?

NO.

ME NEITHER.

WHAT DO YOU THINK OF US TOGETHER?

DRINK UP!

DRINK!

DRINK!

13

I LEFT HIM ONCE.

I LEFT HIM FOR THREE DAYS. WE'D BEEN TOGETHER FOR A WEEK.

HE DIDN'T SPEAK A WORD FOR THOSE THREE DAYS. YOU MUST REALIZE THAT HE'S THE GABBIEST PERSON I KNOW.

AS FOR ME, I NO LONGER RECALL WHAT I DID. I BELIEVE I WAS TERRIBLY BORED.

WHY DID YOU DO THAT?

HE TALKED TOO MUCH. HE LOVED ME TOO MUCH.

JUST A KID, HE WAS ALREADY IN LOVE WITH ME.

AND I FANCIED ANOTHER BOY, TOO.

ONE WHO TALKED LESS?

I DIDN'T EVEN GO SEE HIM DURING THOSE THREE DAYS.

YOU DON'T REGRET IT A LITTLE?

IT WAS KIDS' STUFF. I WAS SIXTEEN.

SIXTEEN! YOU'VE BEEN WITH YOUR SAILOR THAT LONG?

TEN YEARS.

AND THE FELLOW WHO TALKED LESS?

EXCUSE ME. I'M BEING A BOOR.

SHALL WE RESUME THE CLASS?

YOUR WRIST MUSTN'T MOVE.

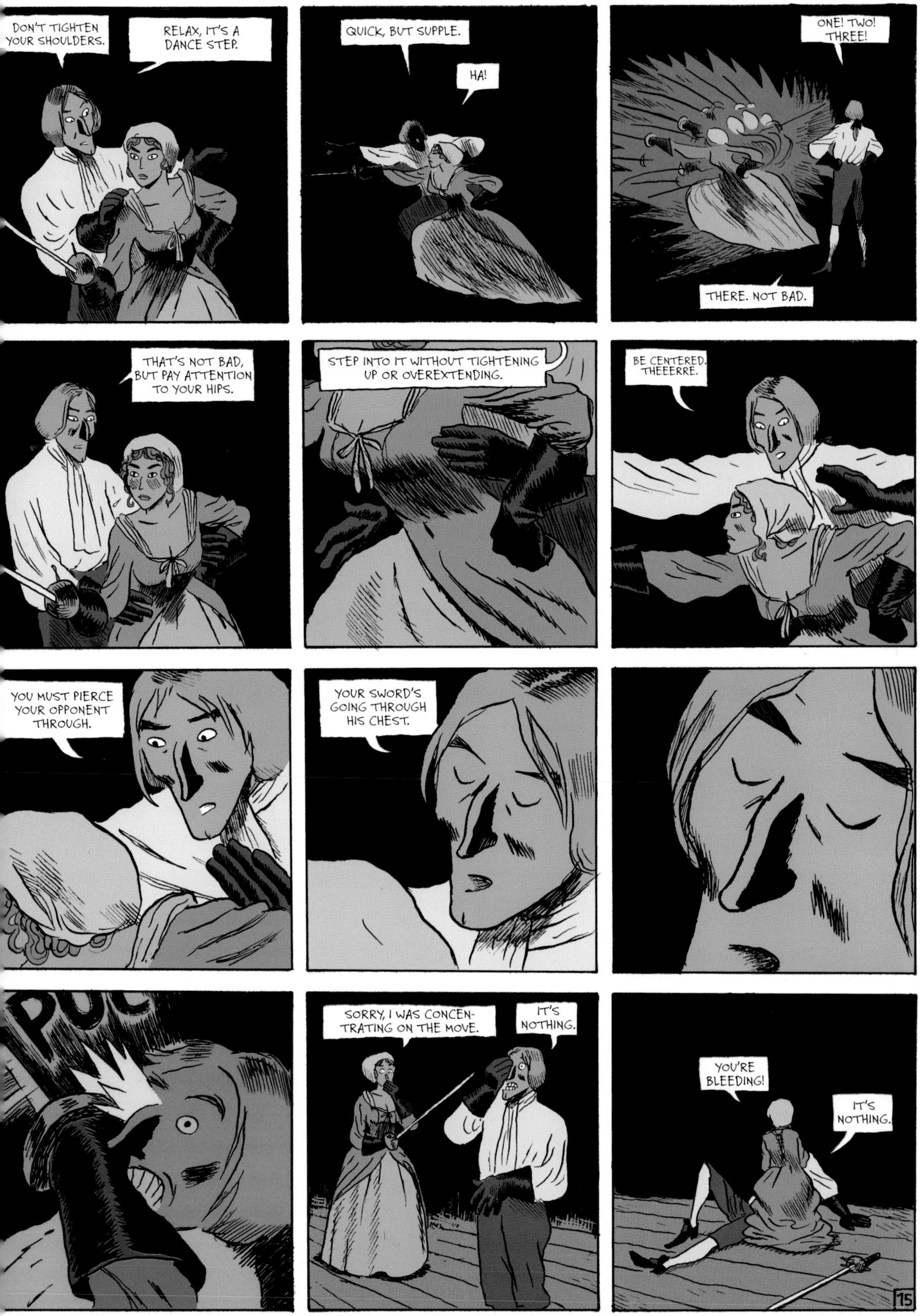
DON'T TIGHTEN YOUR SHOULDERS.
RELAX, IT'S A DANCE STEP.
QUICK, BUT SUPPLE.
HA!
ONE! TWO! THREE!
THERE. NOT BAD.
THAT'S NOT BAD, BUT PAY ATTENTION TO YOUR HIPS.
STEP INTO IT WITHOUT TIGHTENING UP OR OVEREXTENDING.
BE CENTERED. THEEERRE.
YOU MUST PIERCE YOUR OPPONENT THROUGH.
YOUR SWORD'S GOING THROUGH HIS CHEST.
SORRY, I WAS CONCENTRATING ON THE MOVE.
IT'S NOTHING.
YOU'RE BLEEDING!
IT'S NOTHING.

DO YOU SEE THAT BLUE? I'VE NEVER SEEN THE AIR SO TRANSPARENT, SO PURE.

IT'S STARTING TO GET REALLY COLD. WE'RE NEARING OUR GOAL.

WAIT. DO YOU SEE THAT?

WELL, DAMN!

?

WHAT IS IT?

SOME ICE.

GRAB IT! GRAB IT! HURRY UP!

GRAB THE ICE!

BUT DRAW, YOU WRETCH, DRAW! WHERE'S YOUR SKETCHPAD? WHERE'S YOUR PENCIL?

I'M NOT WORKING TODAY.

WHAT?

IT'S A JEWISH HOLIDAY AND I MUSTN'T DO ANYTHING OTHER THAN PRAY AND MEDITATE.

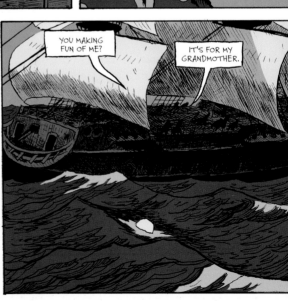

YOU MAKING FUN OF ME?

IT'S FOR MY GRANDMOTHER.

MY GRANDMOTHER RAISED ME AND SHE DIED LAST YEAR.

IF SHE WERE HERE, SHE'D HAVE TAKEN OVER COMMAND. YOUR MEN WOULD'VE MADE HER THEIR MOTHER AND WOULD'VE FEARED HER.

AS FOR YOU, YOU'D WORRY TO DEATH FROM GUILT OVER YOUR PAST VILLAINIES.

DAMN YA! I AIN'T HERE TO BE BUGGED BY GRANDMAS!

JOHN! COME SEE!

AN ICE BLOCK, FOR PETE'S SAKE! IT'S AN ICE BLOCK!

JOHN! THERE ARE LOTS MORE OVER HERE!

IT'S FRESH WATER! FROZEN WATER FROM THE SEA TRANSFORMS INTO FRESH WATER.

IT'S NOT A PIECE OF FROZEN SEA, BUT SURELY A BIT OF ICE FROM YOUR NEW CONTINENT.

HEY, PAINTER! PAINTER! COME LOOK AT THIS!

YOU'RE DRAWING NOW?

DRAWING ISN'T WORK. IT'S A FORM OF PRAYER.

AND I'M BORED.

??

DID YOU SEE? THERE'S ICE EVERYWHERE.

17

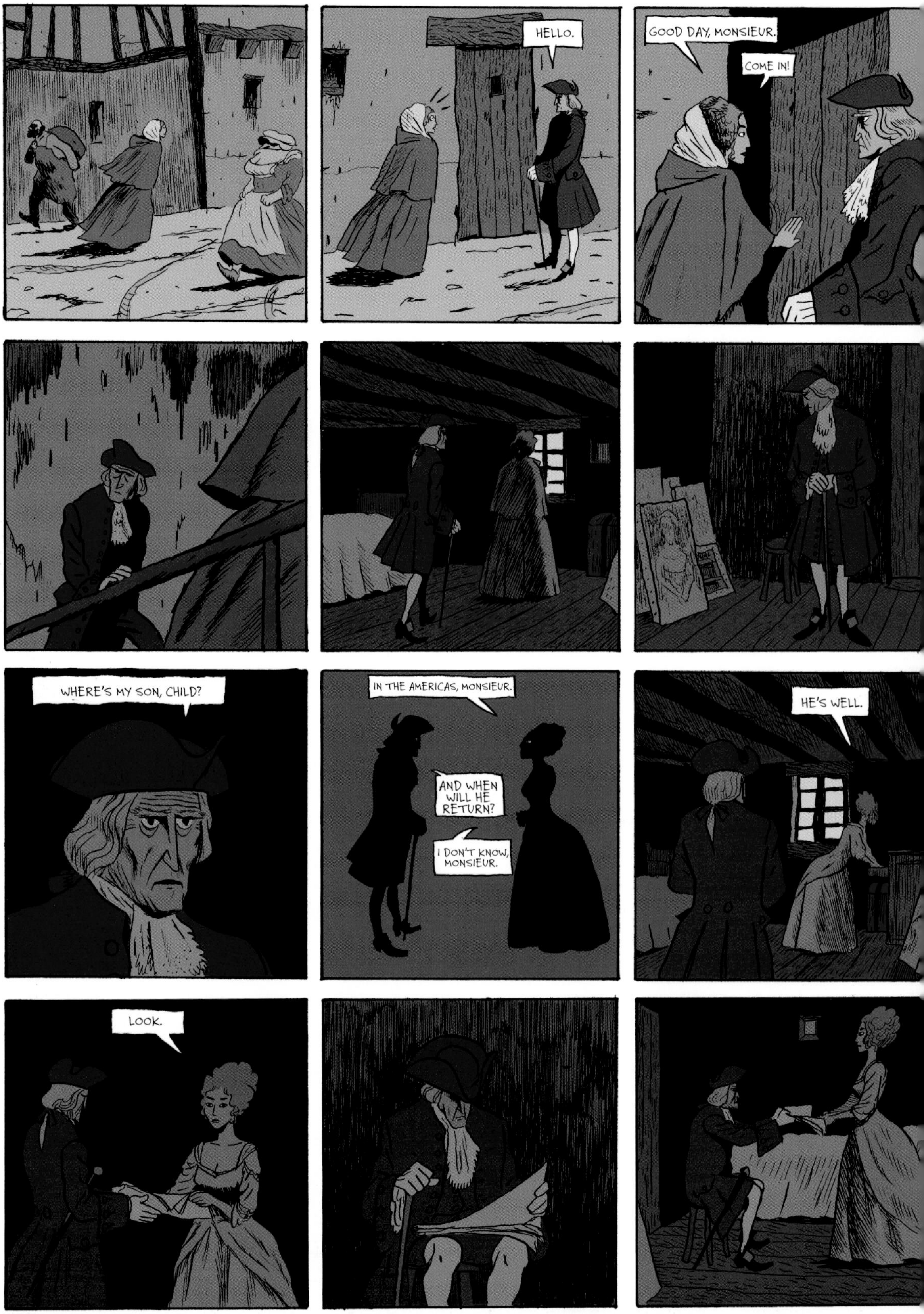
HELLO.
GOOD DAY, MONSIEUR.
COME IN!
WHERE'S MY SON, CHILD?
IN THE AMERICAS, MONSIEUR.
AND WHEN WILL HE RETURN?
I DON'T KNOW, MONSIEUR.
HE'S WELL.
LOOK.

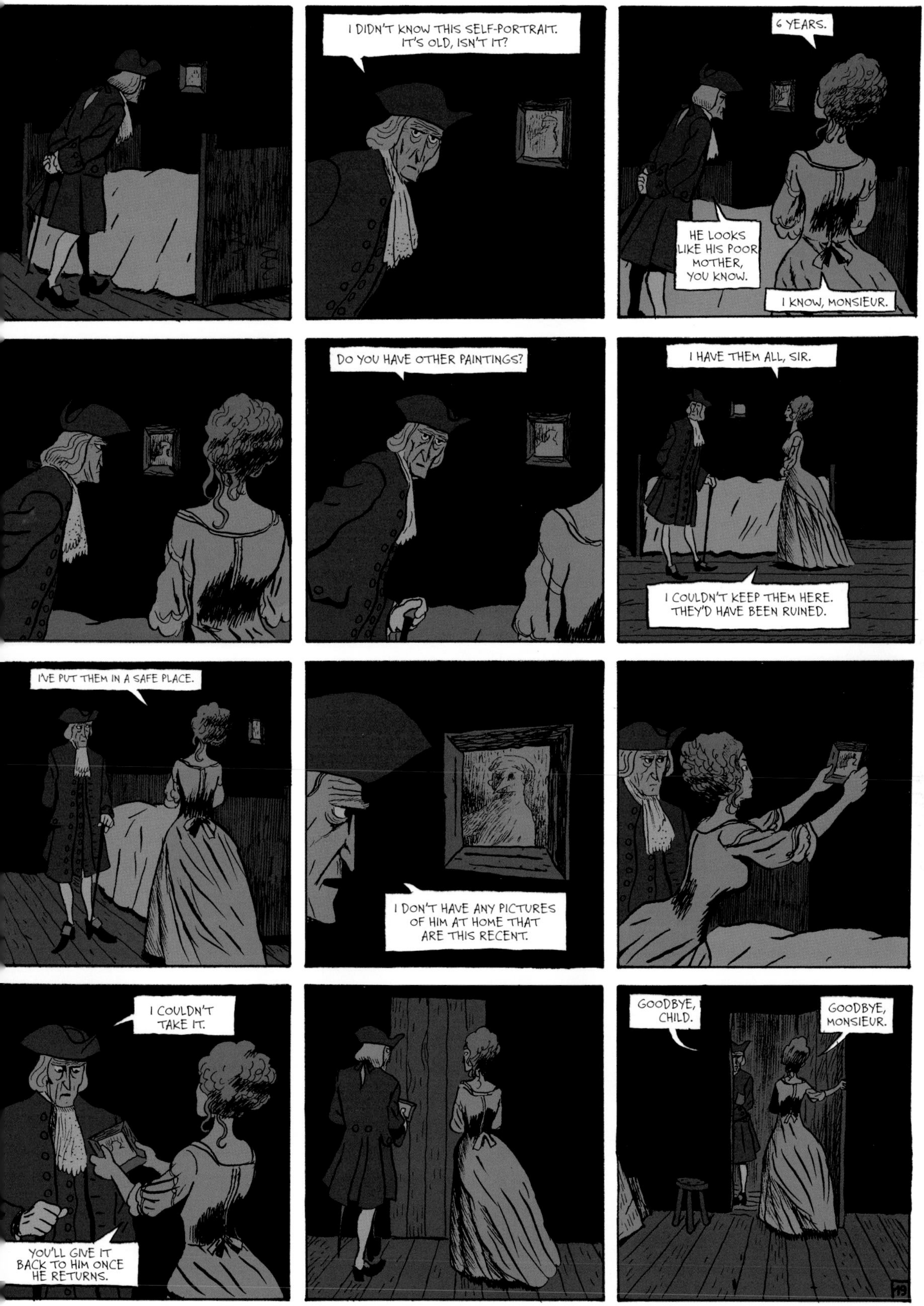
I DIDN'T KNOW THIS SELF-PORTRAIT. IT'S OLD, ISN'T IT?
6 YEARS.
HE LOOKS LIKE HIS POOR MOTHER, YOU KNOW.
I KNOW, MONSIEUR.
DO YOU HAVE OTHER PAINTINGS?
I HAVE THEM ALL, SIR.
I COULDN'T KEEP THEM HERE. THEY'D HAVE BEEN RUINED.
I'VE PUT THEM IN A SAFE PLACE.
I DON'T HAVE ANY PICTURES OF HIM AT HOME THAT ARE THIS RECENT.
I COULDN'T TAKE IT.
YOU'LL GIVE IT BACK TO HIM ONCE HE RETURNS.
GOODBYE, CHILD.
GOODBYE, MONSIEUR.

MMM....WHAT'S THAT?

WHAT'S HAPPENING?

WE BUMPED INTO SOMETHING!!

CHUNKS OF ICE!

PAINTER! COME LOOK AT THIS! COME LOOK AT THIS!

MY SKETCHPAD? WHERE'S MY SKETCHPAD?

DAMN, IT'S COLD!

IT'S MOVING! IT'S COMING TOWARDS US!

NO! LOOK! IT'S GOING BACK THAT WAY!

JOHN!

WHAT?

THE DEAD? THAT'S WHERE THEY GO.

WHAT ARE YOU TALKING ABOUT?!

JOHN, DO YOU THINK IT'S A GOOD OR A BAD SIGN?

BONHOMME OBSERVED THIS SINGULAR EVENT. HA! HA! HIS WHOLE CREW SHUT THEMSELVES UP IN THE HOLD, IN A FIT OF TERROR. I SEE THAT YOU'RE BRAVER, BOYS! HAHAHAHAHA!

SHHH, HENRY!

DO YOU KNOW THAT MISTER HALLEY, A GREAT OBSERVER OF THE SKIES, CLAIMS THAT THIS LUMINOUS PHENOMENON IS CONNECTED WITH STORMS?

HENRY!

DRAW IT!

I DON'T HAVE A SKETCHPAD WITH ME!

DO SOMETHING! GO FIND ONE, QUICK! LOOKS TO ME LIKE IT'S LEAVING!

2.1

HA HA!

ALICE.

YOUR MIND'S ELSE-
WHERE, CHEMIN VERT.

YOU'RE RIGHT, BRISSAC.
I'LL COME BACK LATER.

ALICE.

ALICE.

ALICE, I...

PHILIP!

PHILIP, IT'S BEEN SO LONG SINCE I LAST SAW YOU. WHAT'S THIS NASTY WOUND?

NO, FRANKLY, MY MIND WON'T BE ON WHATEVER I'M DOING TODAY. THIS GAME WILL BE FAR MORE INTERESTING WITHOUT ME.

AS YOU WISH, PAL.

ALICE.

ALICE I...

PHILIP?!

HMM

GOOD EVENING, ALICE. EVERYTHING OKAY?

EVENING, MONSIEUR.

LET'S CELE-BRATE, ALICE

WHAT?

THIS. YOUR WORK. THANKS TO YOU, I'LL BUILD MYSELF A PALACE IN MASULIPATAM.

EH?

IN MASULIPATAM. I SAW IT ON A MAP YESTERDAY; I LIKED THE SOUND OF IT.

HEY, I'LL BRING BACK TIGERS FOR THE ZOOLOGICAL SOCIETY.

THE PROBLEM'S THAT I GOT TO GET THERE BY BOAT.

DO YOU KNOW THAT I SUFFER FROM AN INCUR-ABLE SEASICKNESS?

DO YOU KNOW OF ANY OTHER MEANS TO GET THERE?

LET'S DINE TOGETHER TONIGHT.

I CAN'T. I HAVE TO SEE MY MOTHER.

YOUR MOTHER CAN WAIT A BIT.

WHAT'S THIS ATTITUDE? DINING WITH YOU IS NOT PART OF MY JOB DESCRIPTION, AS FAR AS I KNOW!

WHAT'S WITH THIS BAD MOOD? I'LL WAIT FOR YOU TO GO SEE YOUR MOTHER.

OKAY?

!

I'M LEAVING YOUR SERVICE.

BECAUSE I TRIED TO KISS YOU?

I'VE BEEN PONDERING IT FOR SOME TIME.

WHAT ARE YOU TALKING ABOUT?

HAHA! YOU'RE A HARD ONE! I WON'T TRY IT AGAIN.

PROMISE!

YOU'RE LEAVING NOW?

ALL YOUR FILES ARE THERE. YOU'LL EASILY FIND SOMEONE TO REPLACE ME.

WHY THIS DRAMA?

DID I OFFEND YOU?

ALICE! WHAT?

ALICE!

FINE, DO AS YOU PLEASE!

ASS!

BOOMF

BITCH!

BOMF

WHO PUT THAT PAINTING HERE?

ME, MY DEAR.

YOU GOT UP, MAMA? YOU KNOW YOU SHOULDN'T GET UP!

IT WASN'T EASY, BUT I MANAGED.

WHY DID YOU PUT IT THERE?

I WANTED TO HAVE A GOOD VIEW OF IT. I WAS STILL PRETTY NICE IN THE PAINTING. ADMITTEDLY HE DID PRETTY ME UP A LITTLE.

WHAT MADE YOU TO BRING OUT THIS ANTIQUE? WHEN ISAAC PAINTED IT, WE HADN'T YET BEEN TOGETHER A YEAR.

I COULDN'T SEE IT WELL BECAUSE IT WAS IN A SHADOW. OVER TIME, I'D BEGUN TO FORGET IT SOME.

DID YOU KNOW THAT OILS HAVE TO BE KEPT IN THE LIGHT? OTHERWISE THEY DARKEN.

A QUICK WIPE, A LITTLE LIGHT, AND THERE YOU GO!

DID YOU BRING HIS DRAWINGS? THEY'RE SO BEAUTIFUL.

MAMA, I'M NOT GOING TO BRING THEM EVERY TIME.

YOU DON'T HAVE ANY NEW ONES? HE'S NOT SENT YOU ANY NEW LETTERS?

YES, HE HAS. HE'S WELL. HE OFTEN MENTIONS YOU.

YOU'VE NOT GOTTEN ANY NEW LETTERS!

IF YOU'D GOTTEN MORE LETTERS FROM ISAAC, YOU'D HAVE MORE DRAWINGS. ISAAC NEVER WRITES WITHOUT DRAWING.

I'M SORRY, MY CHILD. COME SIT BESIDE YOUR MAMA.

DON'T POUT. YOU LIKE TO POUT. YOU'VE ALWAYS POUTED.

HOW DO YOU DO IT? I'D GET BORED IF I POUTED LIKE YOU DO.

YOU DON'T TALK MUCH ABOUT ISAAC ANY-MORE. IS THERE ANOTHER FELLOW?

IF THERE'S ANOTHER BOY, I UNDER-STAND, MY DEAR. BUT WHEN ISAAC COMES BACK, YOU WON'T SAY ANY-THING TO HIM, WILL YOU? NEVER!

NEVER, MY DEAR!

BROM BROM

HEY THERE! WHAT ARE YOU LOOKING AROUND FOR, PAINTER?

A SKETCH-PAD.

YOU'VE GOT BOOKS AND DRAWING PAPER ALL OVER!

NO, I WANT THAT BLACK PAD BOUND IN LEATHER.

SOME BASTARD STOLE IT!

DON'T MAKE A BIG DEAL OF IT. NOW'S NOT THE TIME. EVERYONE'S IN A STATE BECAUSE OF THE GREEN LIGHT.

ALSO, FOLKS ARE AFRAID OF RUN-NING INTO A BIG CHUNK OF ICE WITH THIS DAMNED FOG.

WHAT'S THERE THAT'S SO IMPORTANT IN YOUR BOOK?

DRAWINGS OF ALICE.

WHO'S THAT?

MY FIANCÉE.

OH YEAH! YOUR WIFE! THE PRETTY GAL DRAWN IN YOUR BOOK, THE ONE WHO LEFT YOU! ALICE! HAHAHAHA!

YOU SEEN IT?

THE PRETTY GAL?

NO, MY SKETCHPAD!

DRAW SOME OTHER PRETTY WOMEN RATHER THAN MOPING.

ONE DAY, I'LL TELL YOU HOW MY GAL CUT OFF TWO OF MY FINGERS. NOW I'M GONNA GO REPLACE JOHN AT THE HELM.

SO? ARE YOU PESTERING FOLKS ABOUT YOUR SKETCHPADS? LOST THE DRAWINGS OF YOUR WIFE? MAKE SOME OTHERS.

THOSE WERE WELL DONE.

LISTEN, OLD BOY. YOU WON'T SEE THAT GAL OF YOURS AGAIN. IT'S OVER. AND SO WHAT? SHE'S NO LONGER WAITING ON YOU. SHE'S FOUND HERSELF ANOTHER FELLOW AND YOU KNOW THAT.

IT'S BEEN TOO LONG SINCE YOU SAW ANY WOMEN, THAT'S ALL.

DO YOU REALLY WANT TO SEE HER AGAIN? TO DO WHAT? THE WORLD'S YOURS NOW. YOU'LL HAVE ALL THE WOMEN YOU WANT. WE'LL BOTH BECOME KINGS.

HEY, MATE?

I'LL FIND HER. I DON'T GIVE A DAMN ABOUT YOUR TALES OF MATES WHO SHARE THEIR WOMEN.

BUT YOU SEE, IN YOUR SKETCHPAD, THERE WEREN'T JUST PORTRAITS OF YOUR WOMAN. THERE WERE THOSE OF THE GIRL AT THE GOVERNOR'S.

IT'S NOT THE DRAWINGS OF YOUR WOMAN THAT YOU'RE MISSING. YOU KNOW HER SO WELL THAT YOU COULD DRAW HER WITH YOUR EYES CLOSED. THE FACE OF THE OTHER ONE ISN'T SO FAMILIAR TO YOU.

YOU'VE FORGOTTEN HER A LITTLE. YOU'D LIKE TO REMEMBER HER BETTER.

GIMME THE PAD BACK!

I DON'T HAVE YOUR SKETCH-PAD. I DON'T GIVE A DAMN ABOUT IT.

YOU TOOK MY PAD TO WANK OFF TO!

WE'LL HELP YOU FIND YOUR SKETCHPAD.

PUFF... HMM... PUFF

DO YOU KNOW THAT MARINERS OF YORE BELIEVED THAT ONCE HAVING PASSED THE EQUATOR, TOWARDS THE SOUTH, THE CLIMATE WOULD HEAT UNTIL THE VERY OCEANS BOILED?

THEY IMAGINED NAVIGATING IN THAT HELLISH BROTH, SURROUNDED BY ENORMOUS, DIABOLICAL, MALICIOUS MONSTERS.

BONHOMME HIMSELF THOUGHT HE'D FIND A ZONE OF TROPICAL CLIMATE BEYOND THE ICE BARRIER.

MAYBE HE WAS RIGHT, HENRY.

I DON'T THINK SO.

GENTLEMEN, I'LL LEAVE YOU. I'M GOING BACK TO LIE DOWN TO TRY TO SLEEP A LITTLE. I SPENT A GOOD PART OF THE NIGHT CALMING SOULS AGITATED BY THE GREEN LIGHT.

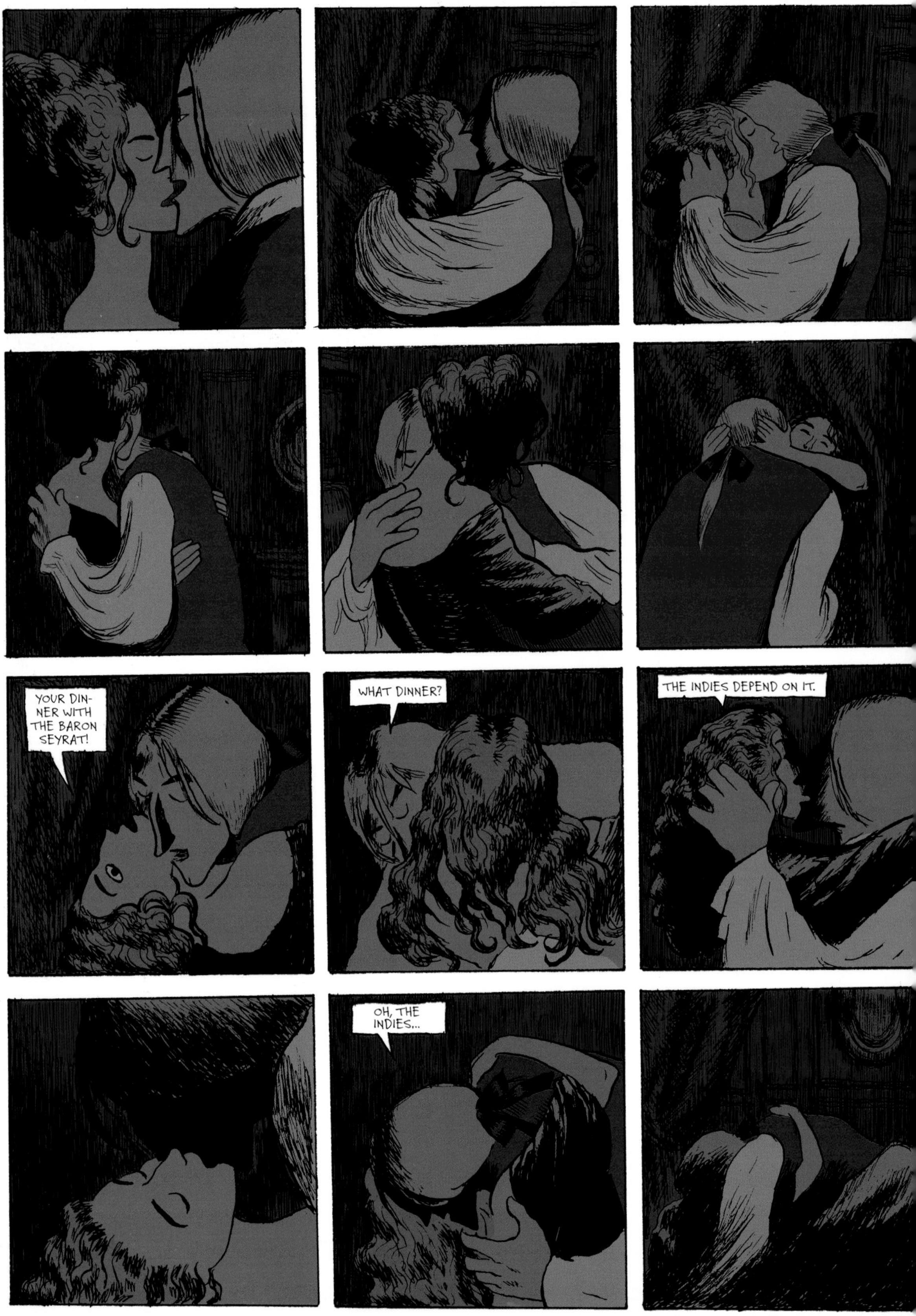
YOUR DINNER WITH THE BARON SEYRAT!
WHAT DINNER?
THE INDIES DEPEND ON IT.
OH, THE INDIES...

IT'S INHABITED.

SOME MEN?

HARD TO SAY. IT LOOKS LIKE IT. THERE! THERE'S SIX OF 'EM. THEY'RE WALKING ON A CLIFF EDGE. I CAN'T TELL WHAT THEY'RE DOING. THEY'RE GONNA FALL OVER!

HAVE THEY SEEN US?

TWO LONGBOATS! TEN ARMED MEN!

YOU, YOU, YOU, AND YOU! GET A SHAVE! EVERYONE LANDING WITH ME WILL SHAVE!

JACK! PREPARE THE BOARDS WITH NAILS!

DON'T WORRY ABOUT MY HEALTH, JOHN. I FEEL JUST FINE AND I WANT TO SET FOOT ON THIS LAND!

WHAT WILL WE CALL THE INHABITANTS OF THIS NEW COUNTRY? "PILLAGERIANS"?

YOU THINK THERE'LL BE ANY PRETTY "PILLAGERIAN" WOMEN?

THIS IS NO JOKING MATTER. IT'S A HISTORIC MOMENT!

THINK ABOUT YOUR WOMAN AND SHUT UP!

THE WATER'S AS THICK AS SOUP!

EASY, BOYS! PUT ON THE BOARDS WITH NAILS FIRST!

IT WAS BONHOMME WHO GOT THIS CLEVER IDEA AFTER HAVING LOST THREE FELLOWS IN THE WATER.

BRRA!

BRRA!

POW

BRRAA!

BRRA!

PLOOOFS

POWDER-KEG, YOU'RE THE BEST SHOT ON BOARD!

WE'LL TAKE IT BACK TO THE BOAT.

DOESN'T SMELL GOOD.

BAH, NO WORSE THAN A PIG.

YOU RECKON IT'S EDIBLE?

THAT'LL BE A CHANGE FROM THE DRIED MEAT.

33

IT'S AN ISLAND!

THERE MUST BE A BIGGER LANDMASS.

OF COURSE, JOHN, BUT WE REALLY ARE ON AN ISLAND!

THIS ISLAND WILL BEAR YOUR NAME, POWDER-KEG, SINCE YOU'RE THE FIRST TO HAVE SEEN IT.

THANKS, JOHN, BUT THE HONOR'S YOURS.

NO, I TOLD YOU THAT I'LL GIVE MY NAME TO THE CONTINENT.

WHO WANTS FOR THIS ISLAND TO BEAR HIS NAME?

YOU, PAINTER, I'VE GOT AN IDEA. GIVE IT YOUR FIANCÉE'S NAME.

I'D RATHER WAIT MYSELF FOR A BIGGER BIT OF LAND. I'M NOT GOING TO NAME JUST ANY OLD ROCK FOR ALICE.

OKAY THEN, GIVE IT THE NAME OF THE GIRL YOU SCREWED AT THE GOVERNOR'S.

IF IT'S IN HISTORY BOOKS, ALICE MIGHT GET SUSPICIOUS.

BUT WHO WOULD KNOW IT WAS YOU WHO CHOSE THAT NAME?

EXCUSE ME, GENTLEMEN, I DON'T THINK THIS IS AN ISLAND.

I DON'T SEE ANY SIGN OF ROCKS. I'M GUESSING RATHER THAT IT'S A GIANT PIECE OF FLOATING ICE, LIKE THOSE THAT WE'VE ENCOUNTERED.

CRACK! AAHH!

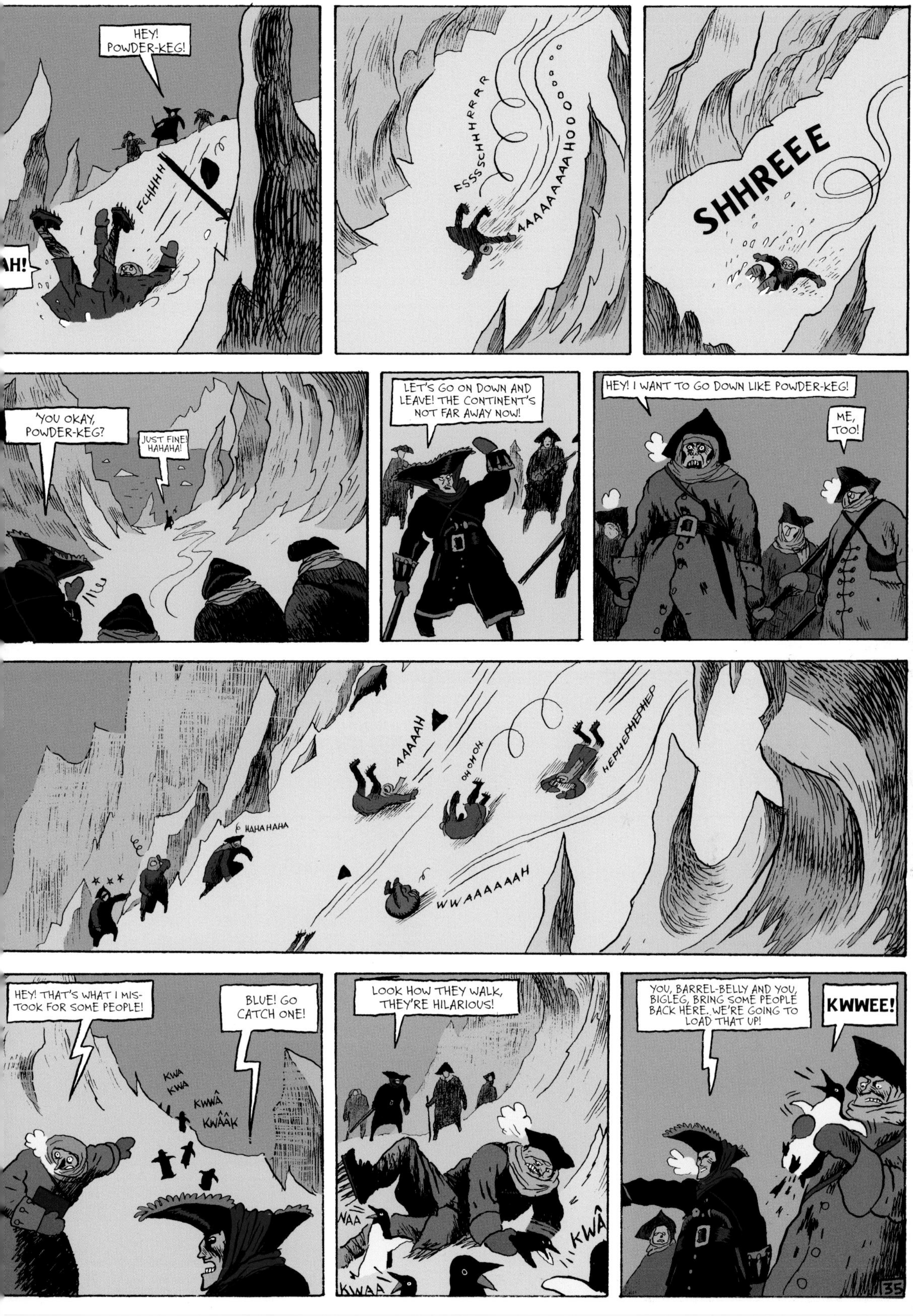

HEY! POWDER-KEG!
FCHHHH
AH!
FSSSCHHHRRRR
AAAAAAAAAHOOOOOOOO
SHHREEE
'YOU OKAY, POWDER-KEG?
JUST FINE! HAHAHA!
LET'S GO ON DOWN AND LEAVE! THE CONTINENT'S NOT FAR AWAY NOW!
HEY! I WANT TO GO DOWN LIKE POWDER-KEG!
ME, TOO!
AAAAAH
HOHOHO
HEPHEPHEPHEP
HAHAHAHA
WWAAAAAAAH
HEY! THAT'S WHAT I MISTOOK FOR SOME PEOPLE!
BLUE! GO CATCH ONE!
KWA KWA
KWÂ
KWÂÂK
LOOK HOW THEY WALK, THEY'RE HILARIOUS!
NAA
KWÂ
KWAA
YOU, BARREL-BELLY AND YOU, BIGLEG, BRING SOME PEOPLE BACK HERE. WE'RE GOING TO LOAD THAT UP!
KWWEE!

I'LL STUDY THIS SPECIMEN BEFORE WE EAT IT.

WE'LL NOT LACK FOR FOOD OR FOR FRESH WATER.

HAHAHAHAHAHAHAHAHAHAHAHAHAHAHAH

ADELIUS! HIS NAME'S ADELIUS! LIKE BARREL-BELLY!

ADELIUS!

KWA KWAKWA!

UH, JOHN?

WHAT, PAINTER?

CAN WE GIVE A WOMAN'S NAME TO THE SEA WHERE WE ARE

CHEMIN VERT, YOU'RE THE BEST AMONG US.

BROGLE ISN'T SO BAD EITHER.

AGAINST CHEMIN VERT? HE'D BETTER THROW DOWN HIS SWORD AND TAKE UP THE CROSS!

HE JUST MIGHT ASK YOU TO TAKE THAT BACK.

I'D PUT MY BOOT IN BROGLE'S ASS, BUT THAT'S NOT THE QUESTION.

YOU'RE MOVING LIKE AN OYSTER, OLD CHAP. YOUR MIND'S ELSEWHERE! FOCUS!

PUSH-OVER!

WELL THEN, BRISSAC, IF THE SWORD NO LONGER SUITS YOU, I COULD ALWAYS PUNCH YOUR LIGHTS OUT.

FOR WHOM DO YOU SO RUDELY ABANDON A CARD GAME?

FOR WHOM ARE YOU GETTING YOUR FACE SMASHED?

DOES SHE HAVE PRETTY TITS?

HER NAME

PHILIP HAS A REAL THING FOR TITS!

HAHAHA! IDIOTS!

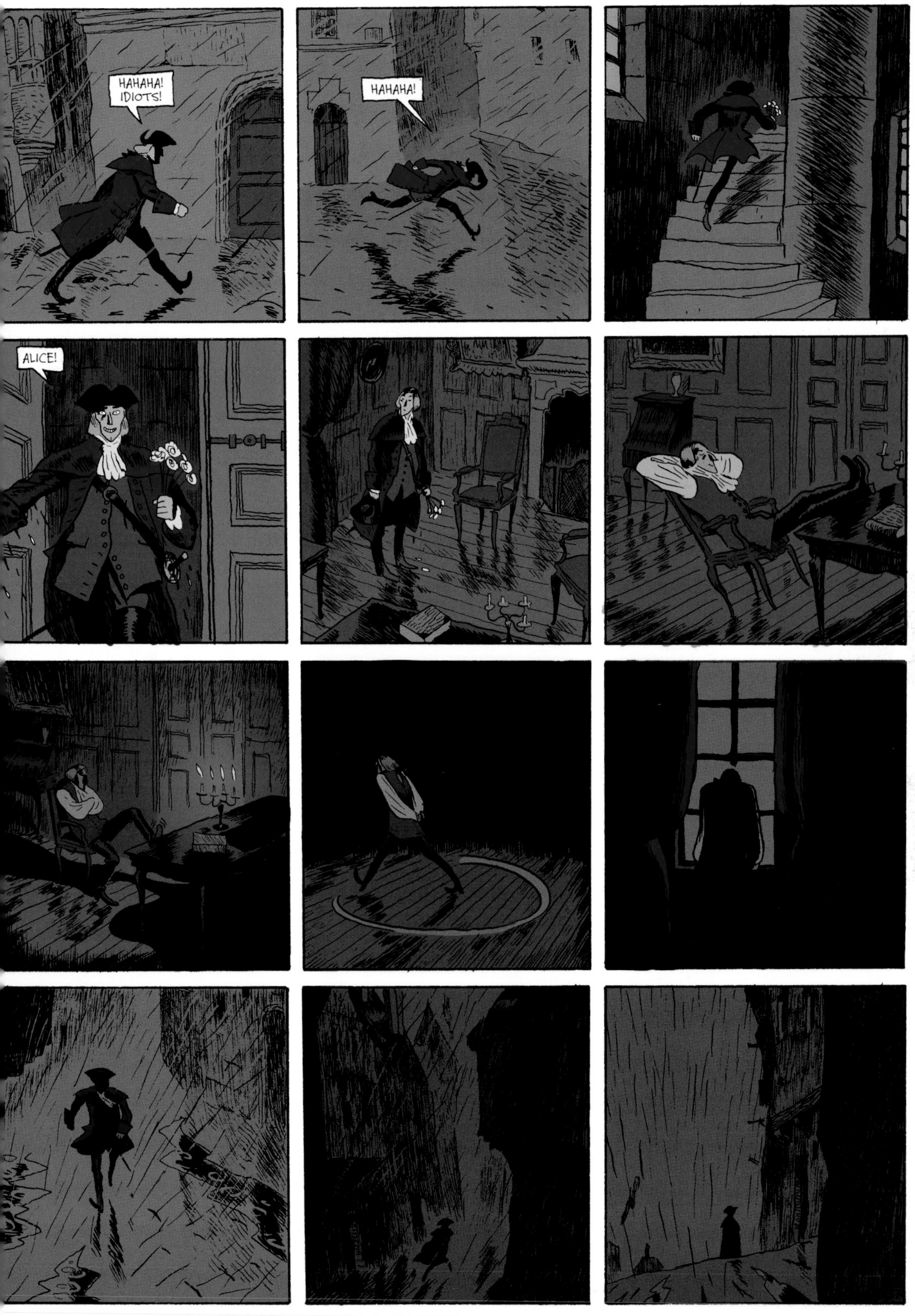
HAHAHA! IDIOTS!
HAHAHA!
ALICE!

AL...

JACK, YOUR STEW IS NASTY.

IT'S THAT BEAST THAT'S ROTTEN! IT'S FLESH IS FATTY, BUT IT HAS A SPOILED SMELL. I TRIED EVERY POSSIBLE SEASONING, BUT IT'S STILL JUST AS DISGUSTING.

LOOK, HENRY'S LOOKING ALL DOWN IN THE FACE FROM EATING YOUR SWILL!

COME NOW! IT'S NOT SO GOOD, BUT I'M MAKING DO.

YOU WANT A PUNCH IN THE SNOUT, JOHN? ARE YOU FINDING US ANY ANIMALS GOOD FOR ROASTING? JUST WHERE ARE YOUR LANDS OF RICHES? LOST IN THE FOG? AND WHERE THE HELL ARE WE?

EXCUSE ME, GENTLEMEN. I'M GOING TO PAY ADELIUS A QUICK VISIT. THE POOR THING'S NOT AT ALL WELL. I THINK HE SORELY MISSES THE COMPANY OF HIS OWN KIND. I'LL LEAVE MY PLATE FOR WHOEVER WANTS TO POLISH IT OFF.

HOW ARE YOU, HENRY? YOU REALLY DO LOOK LIKE YOU'RE TIRED.

I'M DOING FINE, MY BOY.

ADELIUS IS THE ONE WHO COULDN'T STAND CAPTIVITY. HE WANDERED ABOUT SO SAD FOR DAYS.

I DON'T HAVE THE HEART TO DISSECT HIM. WE'LL FIND PLENTY OTHERS OF HIS KIND.

PLOF

ADELIUS IS DEAD!

ADELIUS IS DEAD!

HEY!

WHAT A STRANGE SHIP!

SOME PILLAGERIANS!

TO ARMS!

CANNONS ARE FROZEN!

SHIT!

JOHN! THE CANNONS ARE USELESS.

39

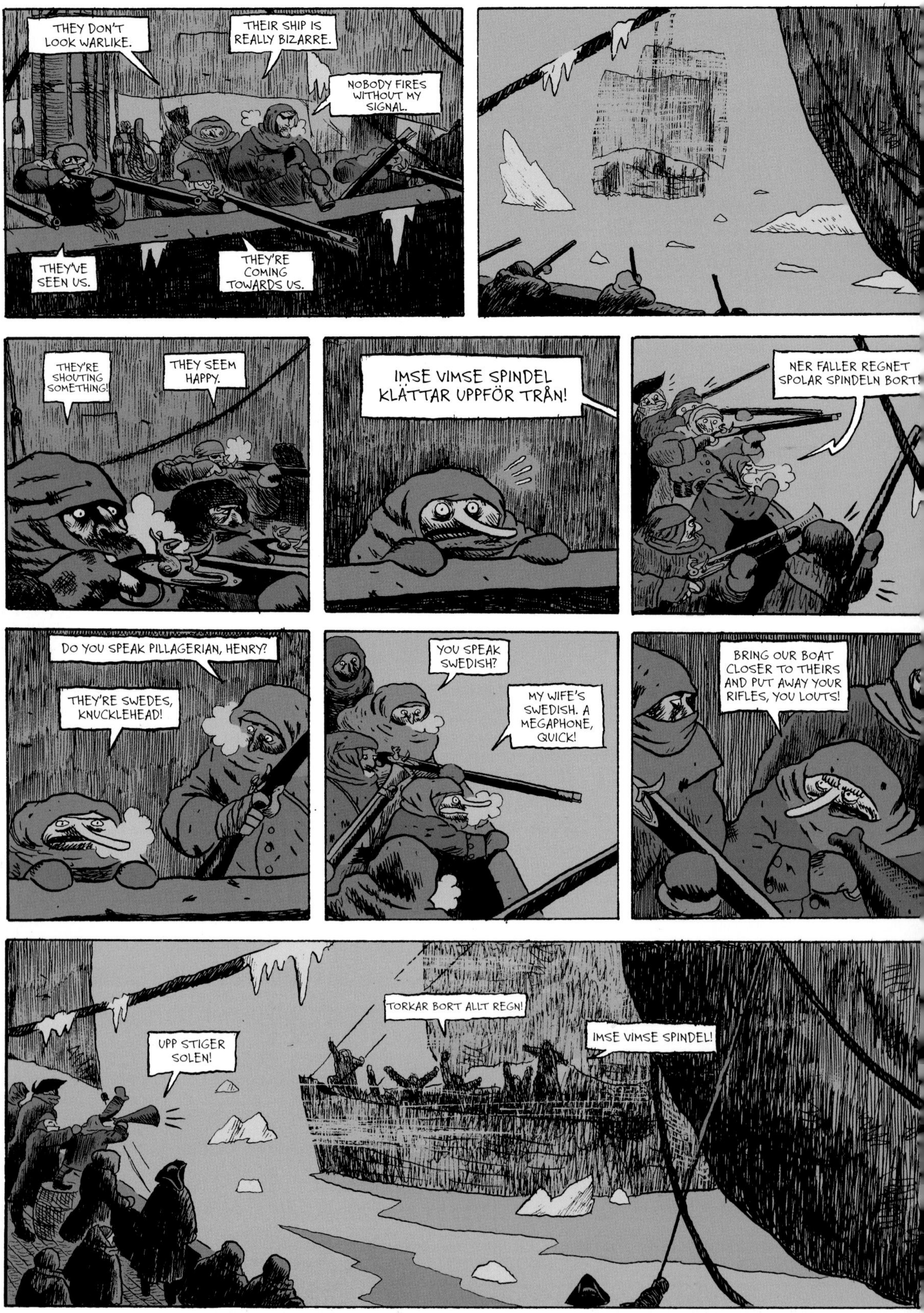
THEY DON'T LOOK WARLIKE.
THEIR SHIP IS REALLY BIZARRE.
NOBODY FIRES WITHOUT MY SIGNAL.
THEY'VE SEEN US.
THEY'RE COMING TOWARDS US.
THEY'RE SHOUTING SOMETHING!
THEY SEEM HAPPY.
IMSE VIMSE SPINDEL KLÄTTAR UPPFÖR TRÅN!
NER FALLER REGNET SPOLAR SPINDELN BORT!
DO YOU SPEAK PILLAGERIAN, HENRY?
THEY'RE SWEDES, KNUCKLEHEAD!
YOU SPEAK SWEDISH?
MY WIFE'S SWEDISH. A MEGAPHONE, QUICK!
BRING OUR BOAT CLOSER TO THEIRS AND PUT AWAY YOUR RIFLES, YOU LOUTS!
UPP STIGER SOLEN!
TORKAR BORT ALLT REGN!
IMSE VIMSE SPINDEL!

BRING THEM ABOARD, FOR GOD'S SAKE!

BOOHOOHOO!

BOOHOOHOO!

BOOOO!

BOOHOO HOOHOO!

IMSE VIMSE SPINDEL!

KLÄTTAR UPP IGEN!

TAKE CARE OF OUR GUESTS! GIVE THEM SOMETHING TO EAT! WARM THEM UP! GO ON! GO ON!

BÄ BÄ VITA LAMM HAR DU NÅGON ULL? JA, HA KÄRA BAM JAG HAR SÄCKEN FULL!

?

HELGDAGSROCK ÅT FAR OGH SÖNDAGS KJOL ÅT MOR OCH TVÅ PAR STUMBAR ÅT LILLE, LILLE BROR!

WHO ARE THESE GUYS?

I DON'T KNOW.

41

HENRY?

GENTLEMEN, WE HAVE TO LEAVE HERE QUICKLY!

OUR SHIP RISKS BEING TRAPPED IN THE ICE LIKE THAT OF THESE WRETCHES.

THE WATER FROZE COMPLETELY, IMMOBILIZING THEIR SHIP NEAR THE CONTINENT. REALIZING THEY'D HAVE TO AWAIT A WARMER SEASON AND THE MELTING OF THE ICE, THEY MADE READY TO WINTER THERE.

BUT THE ICE CRUSHED THEIR SHIP, FORCING THEM TO ATTEMPT TO SURVIVE ON THE COASTS.

THEY DUG OUT TUNNELS IN THE ICE AND LIVED THERE SHELTERED FROM THE UNENDING TEMPESTS.

...HE AMONG THEM SET OUT IN RECONNAISSANCE PARTIES TO THE FURTHEST BOUNDS OF THIS SEA OF ICE.

BOM! BOM!

?

CRAC!

THEY NEVER RETURNED.

THEY RECOVERED WHAT THEY COULD FROM THE WRECKAGE OF THEIR SHIP AND COBBLED TOGETHER THE SHIP IN WHICH WE FOUND THEM.

THE ICE WAS CONTINUING TO FORM FROM THE CONDENSATION IN THE TUNNELS, ALMOST FORCING THEM TO CRAWL ABOUT.

...HE NIGHT, THREE QUARTERS OF THE TUNNELS COL-LPSED LEAVING ONLY THE SURVIVORS THAT WE MET.

WELL, JUST IMAGINE, GENTLEMEN, THAT DESPITE THIS GLACIAL HELL, THESE SWEDES NEVER CEASED TO KEEP ALIVE THEIR SCIENTIFIC CURIOSITY. THEY CARRIED OUT THEIR EXPERIMENTS AS WELL AS THEY COULD, STUDYING THE FAUNA, THE TERRAIN, AND EVEN THE SKY.

THEIR RESEARCH DISAPPEARED IN THE TUNNEL COLLAPSE AND ONLY ONE OF THEIR SCIENTISTS HAS SURVIVED. HE'S IN SUCH A STATE OF EXHAUSTION THAT HE WAS UNABLE TO SPEAK TO ME VERY CLEARLY. I DID UNDERSTAND THAT HE'D COMMITTED THE BULK OF THEIR DISCOV-ERIES TO MEMORY. I HOPE TO GET HIM BACK ON HIS FEET SOON.

HE SPOKE OF THINGS THAT CAME FROM THE SKY BURIED IN THE ICE....OF BRETHREN TO ADELIUS AS BIG AS MEN GATHERED BY THE THOUSANDS. HAHAHA! IMAGINE THAT! HAHAHA!

HENRY!

OH, DAMN!

I CAN'T REMEMBER HER FACE ANY LONGER.

I SAW MY DAUGHTER'S FACE. SHE WAS ALL GROWN UP. SHE'S GROWN UP NOW. WHEN I LEFT HER, SHE WAS THAT LITTLE. I'VE NEVER SEEN HER GROWN UP. I JUST SAW HER AND I CAN NO LONGER RECALL HER FACE. I DIDN'T EVEN SPEAK TO HER.

UH, IS THAT THE DAUGHTER YOU HAD WITH YOUR SWEDISH WIFE?

WHY YES! YES! YOU KNEW THAT? MY WIFE IS VERY BEAUTIFUL. TALL AND VERY BEAUTIFUL. YOU CAN'T IMAGINE ME WITH SUCH A WOMAN, CAN YOU? MY DAUGHTER'S VERY BEAUTIFUL, TOO.

EXCUSE ME.

WHAT COMFORT I FELT WHEN I SAW THAT MY DAUGHTER DIDN'T LOOK LIKE ME! SHE WAS ADORABLE! HER NAME'S ISABELLE.

HOW OLD IS SHE?

SHE MUST BE TWELVE YEARS OLD NOW. SHE'S SURELY TALLER THAN HER FATHER. HAHAHA!

I RETURNED TO PARIS TO SEE HER. THAT'S WHERE I MET YOU.

DID YOU WANT TO SEE YOUR WIFE AGAIN?

OH! I WASN'T EXPECTING ANYTHING FROM HER! I'D MARRY HER A SECOND TIME, IF I COULD. I'D MARRY HER TEN TIMES, BUT I WASN'T EXPECTING MUCH! I HAD LOTS OF MONEY WITH ME, MONEY EARNED WITH JOHN. I WAS SAVING IT FOR ISABELLE.

I LOST TRACK OF HER. I ONLY KNOW THAT MY WIFE REMARRIED. I HEARD THAT HE WAS WEALTHY. THAT'S GOOD.

NOW, THEY BOTH THINK I'M DEAD.

HMM, WHY DID YOU LEAVE THEM?

I FLED, OLD BOY.

I HAD A MISTRESS. OH, NOTHING BAD UP TILL THEN, BUT MY MISTRESS'S HUSBAND WAS ONE OF THOSE JEALOUS, MURDEROUS IMBECILES. HE CAUGHT US, HIS SWORD IN HAND.

I NEGOTIATED, BUT IN VAIN. NOT CONTENT WITH BEING AN IDIOT, HE WAS DRUNK. I KILLED HIM. HE WAS SOMEONE OF SOME IMPORTANCE, SO I FLED.

I BECAME A WRETCHED DOCTOR IN THE MERCHANT MARINE (THEY DON'T ASK QUESTIONS ABOUT YOUR PREVIOUS LIFE IN THE MERCHANT MARINE, PRETTY HANDY). I WAS A VERY GOOD DOCTOR BEFORE, YOU KNOW? PEOPLE WOULD ASK FOR ME FROM FAR AWAY. THEY'D EVEN COME TO MY HOME.

MY SHIP RAN INTO JOHN'S AND THERE YOU HAVE IT...HAHAHA! THAT'S ENOUGH! I'LL TELL YOU MORE ABOUT IT SOME TIME.

ARE YOU MAD AT ME FOR BRINGING YOU ALONG ON THIS?

TELL ME THE STORY THAT JACK LIKES SO MUCH.

YOU KNOW, WITH YOUR FIANCÉE.

OH YES! ALICE LEFT ME WHEN WE WERE SIXTEEN YEARS OLD.

"IT'D BEEN A WEEK SINCE SHE'D PROMISED ME HER LOVE. SHE TOOK IT BACK." "WHY'S THAT?" "I LOVED HER TOO MUCH. IT SCARED HER."

"I DIDN'T EAT OR SPEAK FOR A MONTH. AN ATTACK OF MUTENESS! MY FATHER AND GRANDMOTHER THOUGHT I WAS GOING TO DIE."

"SO?" "SO SHE CAME BACK AFTER THAT MONTH. AT THE VERY MOMENT WHEN I REALIZED IT, I WAS BACK ON MY FEET. I'D FORGOTTEN EVERYTHING."

I DON'T KNOW WHY JACK LIKES THAT STORY. IT MAKES HIM LAUGH A LOT EVERY TIME.

ESPECIALLY THE ATTACK OF MUTENESS.

LIKE THIS.

HA HA HA HA!

LET'S TRY TO SLEEP, MY FRIEND.

95

Christophe Blain

TO BE CONTIN